Narcissism Exposed

Breaking the Self-Destructive Patterns of Self-Idolatry and Self-Exaltation

PATRICIA KING

Narcissism Exposed

Patricia King

BONUS BOOK: God Loves You With An Everlasting Love

Distributed by Patricia King Ministries
P. O. Box 1017
Maricopa, Arizona 85139
PatriciaKing.com

ISBN: 978-1-62166–531-1

TABLE OF CONTENTS

NARCISSISM EXPOSED

BONUS BOOK:

GOD LOVES YOU...
WITH AN EVERLASTING LOVE

DEDICATED TO

All my friends and co-laborers
who embrace the values of
humility, servanthood, faith and selfless love…
yes, **LOVE.**

INTRODUCTION

I sometimes like watching crime shows that reveal the conquering of lawlessness and the establishment of justice. Some episodes I've watched portray situations where a narcissistic sociopath is pursued, arrested, tried, convicted and sentenced.

I realized as I watched these programs that I knew little about the subject of narcissism, so I decided to engage in a study just out of curiosity. Through my research I discovered that narcissism is not confined to sociopathic murderers but can also manifest in people who have never broken civil or federal laws. I found that there are both mild and severe symptoms, but all of it is fueled with self-exaltation, pride, self-absorption and self-focus.

During my season of research, information regarding narcissistic behavior seemed to be heralded in news headlines and broadcasts, in books and internet articles on a regular basis. Television programs such as "American Greed," "Lifestyles of the Rich and Famous," "Forensic Files," and others have revealed narcissism manifesting in almost every sector of society. In many reality programs, narcissism is also clearly modeled. Through these exposures, self-exalting and self-fulfilling perspectives and behaviors have in many ways become normalized.

Everywhere I looked, narcissism was there in front of me. In reviewing certain scenarios, I became aware that in the church I could see patterns and symptoms of this disorder running rampant, yet it was not being identified, confronted or conquered. Many have noted an increase of narcissistic behaviors in the church and even amongst Christian leaders. However, narcissism is not confined to any sphere of influence. You will also find people influenced in home and family settings, in the workplace, in schools, and in government.

In many ways, you could say it has become an epidemic that is not confined to any age group or gender. As a result, criminology, sociology and psychology professors around the world are educating their students regarding this disorder. The more I researched, the more I realized that the world has few solutions and very little hope. But what does the Bible say? What does God say?

In the following pages, I will attempt to briefly unpack some revelation regarding narcissism: what it is and how to overcome it. With Christ all things are possible.

Love is the weapon and the force that will take out this destructive entity. Love is a person – Jesus Christ. Love – His pure, selfless love is our hope and our victory!

CHAPTER ONE

WHAT IS NARCISSISM?

NARCISSISM – THE MYTH

The word *narcissism* comes from the Greek myth of Narcissus, who was a very attractive young man, loved and admired by many. He was renowned for his beauty and was greatly favored, attracting attention wherever he went and in whatever he did. In various versions of the myth, he is portrayed as exceptionally cruel in that he eventually despised and rejected those who had loved him and given their full attention and heart to him. Narcissus invited the adoration and praise given him by all, but he himself loved no one and never reciprocated the love given to him. In his own eyes, there was no one equal to him or truly worthy of him.

The myth portrays the destructive patterns and cycles of self-admiration. Narcissus was unable to love or connect with anyone outside himself, and the rejection he gave to others *severely hurt those who loved him*.

In the myth, Echo (a wood nymph who because of a curse could only repeat words that were spoken to her) fell deeply in love with

Narcissus and longed to be noticed and adored by him. The dream of her heart was for Narcissus to take notice of her, claiming her as his own forever. In order to gain his affection, she would go to any length to please and serve him.

One day while in the woods, Narcissus called out to her, inviting her to join him. Echo was delighted. Narcissus had noticed her and called her to himself! Finally her inner longings were being realized. She ran towards him and threw herself upon him. She wholeheartedly gave herself to him, but in return Narcissus cruelly rejected her and threw her to the ground with repulsion and walked away.

Echo left the woods devastated, ashamed, brokenhearted and crushed in spirit. She lived alone in the mountain ranges for the rest of her days. Daily she longed and pined for a love that would never be returned. She finally died of grief and loneliness, and her body became one with the mountain stone. All that was left was her voice that echoed what others spoke.

Narcissus continued to attract the attention and love of many nymphs. He would entertain them for a season, receiving their attention and adoration, and then would ultimately reject each one. The gods disliked the way he was treating others and as a result cursed him forever. They wanted him to know what it felt like to love and never be loved in return.

One day, while walking in the forest, he came upon a small lake, as smooth as glass. As he gazed into the pool, he saw a beautiful image of himself, although he did not recognize his own reflection. He was captivated by the image he saw. Never had he felt such personal attraction! Never had he felt love like this. As he bent down to kiss the vision, he noticed that the reflection copied his actions. This intensified his intrigue and emotional longings. He had finally found someone who was one with him, someone he could truly admire and love! He reached into the reflection to draw the image to himself, thinking it was a water spirit. As he touched the water, the reflection disappeared. He was distraught and panicked, wondering where his love had gone. When the water became calm, the reflection returned. He cried out to the reflection, "Oh, beautiful one, where did you go? Why did you leave me?"

He once more reached out to touch the one he loved. As his hands touched the water, the image disappeared again. He became fearful and no longer wanted to touch the water, as he did not want the one he longed for to leave him. He lay on the bank of the pool gazing into the eyes of the reflection but was unable to connect. He pined by the hour and refused to eat or drink. At first, many came around to comfort and encourage him. Others offered counsel to help him overcome, but he rejected each one. After many days and numerous failed attempts, they all left him. As time went on, he withered away, becoming emaciated and losing his beauty. He eventually died all alone in severe grief and loneliness on the banks of the pond. His body disappeared and a flower now known as the narcissus (a species of daffodil) grew in its place.

The story of Echo and Narcissus portrays the deception, trap and ultimate tragedy and destruction of self-idolatry. It also reveals the pain and grief of those who love someone who cannot, or will not, reciprocate that love.

LUCIFER, THE ULTIMATE NARCISSIST

Lucifer was the ultimate narcissist and ultimate enemy to God and His Kingdom. He was the anointed covering cherub, created the most beautiful being in heaven and given a position of influence and honor (see Ezekiel 28:14). He lived in a perfect environment of love, blessing, purity and glory, yet he chose to sin and he invited the worship and focus of all unto himself. He exalted himself above God and all He created. Lucifer became completely self-absorbed, self-focused, self-exalting and self-fulfilling – the main characteristics of narcissism. A clear profile of narcissism is evidenced in the scriptural study of the behavior and actions of Lucifer.

Isaiah 14:13-14 gives us a glimpse into Lucifer's exalted heart, "But you said in your heart, 'I will ascend to heaven; I will raise my throne above the stars of God, and I will sit on the mount of assembly in the recesses of the north. I will ascend above the heights of the clouds; I will make myself like the Most High.'"

In Ezekiel 28:12-17 the Scripture further confirms that Lucifer, the anointed covering cherub, was created the most beautiful, most gifted and most blessed of all, yet he chose to arrogantly exalt himself above God.

"Thus says the Lord God, 'You had the seal of perfection, full of wisdom and perfect in beauty. You were in Eden, the garden of God; every precious stone was your covering: the ruby, the topaz and the diamond; the beryl, the onyx and the jasper; the lapis lazuli, the turquoise and the emerald; and the gold, the workmanship of your settings and sockets, was in you. On the day that you were created they were prepared. You were the anointed cherub who covers, and I placed you there. You were on the holy mountain of God; you walked in the midst of the stones of fire. You were blameless in your ways from the day you were created until unrighteousness was found in you. By the abundance of your trade you were internally filled with violence, and you sinned; therefore I have cast you as profane from the mountain of God. And I have destroyed you, O covering cherub, from the midst of the stones of fire. Your heart was lifted up because of your beauty; you corrupted your wisdom by reason of your splendor. I cast you to the ground; I put you before kings, that they may see you.'"

THE BEHAVIOR, THE DISORDER, AND THE DEMON

Narcissistic behaviors and symptoms are noted in the next chapter. Every individual can potentially fall into some level of these behaviors from time to time as they are symptomatic of our fallen nature. In order to mature as a healthy individual, it is important to identify those behaviors and deal with them, as you will see in a later section of the book. Manifesting narcissistic behavior does not mean you have a disorder and or that you are controlled by a demonic entity.

Narcissistic Personality Disorder (NPD), on the other hand, is a medical diagnosis given to a behavioral and social disorder based on the symptoms, effects and consequences of extreme self-focus and self-idolatry. It involves egotistical pursuits, offering self-gratification, dominance and ambition to the exclusion of others. The name of the disorder is taken from the previously mentioned Greek myth of Narcissus and Echo.

The Mayo Clinic offers the following description: "Narcissism is a disorder in which people have an inflated sense of their own importance and have a deep need for admiration. Those with Narcissistic Personality Disorder believe that they're superior to others and have little regard for other people's feelings. But behind this 'mask' of ultra-confidence lies a fragile self-esteem, vulnerable to the slightest criticism."

When an individual fails to deal with narcissistic behaviors and choices over time, demonic oppression and control becomes an issue. Whenever an individual "creates a landing strip" for the enemy through sinful choices, they are opening the door of their life to possible demonic assault and control. Demon possession and oppression are very real, and we see it clearly in the New Testament. Jesus taught about two invisible kingdoms in the unseen dimension – the kingdom of God and the kingdom of Satan (Luke 8:1; John 14:30). Jesus also cast out devils and empowered and commissioned His disciples to do the same (see Mark 16:17; Matthew 10:8).

We are a three-part being (spirit, soul, and body) and when we are born again, our spirit is born again (John 3:6) and we become a brand new creation – old things have passed away and all things have become new (2 Corinthians 5:17). Jesus clearly taught that it is our spirit that is born again, not our soul or body. Our soul is being renewed by the Word of God and our physical bodies will be replaced with a glorious body one day. Our soul and body have been purchased but are not yet perfect. It is very evident that following the born-again experience, all things in our soul (mind, will, emotions) and our body have not become new. However, in our spirits, all things are new and old things are passed away. Our born-again spirit cannot have a demon, sickness, disease, or sin. Our spirit is holy and pure and it is where God dwells within us by His Spirit. We are called to live out this glorious life by faith. We do not have to strive to obtain this life, it is already in us when we receive Christ as our Savior. This is the glorious miracle of rebirth. When we embrace our new identity, by faith, the new "God-nature" flows from our innermost being like a river and fills our soul and body.

Although Christians cannot be demonized in their spirit, it is possible for believers to be oppressed and controlled by demonic spirits in their soul and body if an individual chooses to give place to the enemy through sin or generational iniquity.

As I shared earlier, Satan, once a beautiful angel named Lucifer, is now fallen from his heavenly position and is God's archenemy for all time. Along with his demonic cohorts who fell into rebellion with him and were cast out of heaven, he prowls around like a roaring lion looking for someone to devour (see 1 Peter 5:8). He is looking for those who will submit to him, that he might rule over them, controlling them with his deception and rebellion and conforming them unto his likeness.

Romans 6:16 teaches us that, "...when you present yourselves to someone as slaves for obedience, you are slaves of the one whom you obey, either of sin resulting in death, or of obedience resulting in righteousness." When you give yourself to sin, you actually grant the enemy legal license to control in the areas you opened to him. Sin is dangerous. The enemy is watching to find those points of legal access so that he might steal, kill and destroy (see John 10:10).

Demons can control a person who is operating in narcissistic behavior. Through the gift of the discerning of spirits (1 Corinthians 12:10), we can identify "spirits of narcissism." We are to expose, identify and annihilate their ungodly assignments through discernment, true repentance and the execution of the power of the name of Jesus. Spirits of narcissism jump on the landing strip of sin and deception. As believers, we are well able to overcome any assignment of the enemy through Christ. In Him, we have power "over all the power of the enemy, and nothing will injure us." (Luke 10:19)

The Nature and Danger of Deception

When you are deceived, you do not know it until the truth is revealed; that is the nature of deception. Deception is different from rebellion. If you were to rebel, you know what is right yet deliberately choose to do what is wrong. When deceived, you actually believe you are right. Deception creates blind spots in your perception so that you cannot actually see the truth. What you believe feels like the truth when you are deceived. Narcissism is rooted in deception. In the myth, when Narcissus looked into the reflection he actually believed with full conviction that it was a true being he could love. It was not true, so he died believing the lie. This is a picture of the nature of deception.

The best safeguard against deception is a good accountability team around you. People who love you enough to speak the truth to you are great gifts, but, of course, their effectiveness depends on your willingness to submit to their wisdom and advice. Narcissus had those around him who tried to comfort him but not those who spoke the truth. I love accountability and I love truth. I listen and submit to the input from my accountability relationships. This is a safeguard against deception. Unfortunately, I know a few who put accountability teams around them but when confrontation came, they dissolved the members who disagreed with them and then surrounded themselves with those who agreed with them or endorsed them. This is the nature of narcissism. The outcome was disastrous as they continued to grow in deception rather than truth. They originally put a team of credible people around them for endorsement and for appearance sake only, but not for true accountability. When confrontation came to challenge some of the behaviors and symptoms that are the fruit of narcissism, they found others of even greater stature to agree with them and to invalidate the ones who confronted. This type of action in response to confrontation is actually a symptom of a spirit of narcissism at work, and it potentially increases its hold on those who succumb to its deception.

QUESTIONS TO PONDER

1. Can you identify any areas and/or seasons in your own life where you may have displayed narcissistic behavior? In what ways? What was the outcome?

2. We see that even though our spirit is immediately transformed, our soul takes time for that transformation. What areas of your own soul are in process?

3. Do you have people who have permission to speak into your own life? Who are they?

4. How do you handle personal correction?

5. Are you aware if your spiritual leadership (pastor, mentor, apostles/prophets and Christian media personalities you follow) has an accountability team? Why is this important?

CHAPTER TWO

THE SYMPTOMS, THE FRUIT AND THE BEHAVIOR

I f you had a family member who was manifesting abnormal and concerning symptoms in their body, you would want to help them discover the problem. You would take them to a medical practitioner to discover the cause. This is called "exposure." You will never be able to apply a solution if the problem is not defined and exposed. For example, if you took your loved one to the doctor and they discovered a cancerous tumor, you wouldn't want to just leave it in the body to grow and possibly metastasize. The doctor would give you a solution: perhaps chemotherapy, radiation, or surgery. However, the doctor would never be able to effectively treat the problem until it is diagnosed. The problem must be exposed first.

Jesus disclosed the importance of exposure to His disciples.

"Everything hidden and covered up will soon be exposed. For the facade is falling down, and nothing will be kept secret for long." (Luke 12:2 TPT)

In this hour the Lord is exposing narcissism in order for healing and freedom to come to the individual bound by it, as well as to those in their life who suffer the effects of it.

In the medical field, diagnosis is made through various means, but one significant and oftentimes conclusive means is to simply note symptoms. How can you discern the presence of narcissism? As in the medical field, observing symptoms is one of the primary ways. Jesus taught, "You will know them by their fruits" (Matthew 7:16).

In addition to simply observing the symptoms and the fruit, believers also have access to a supernatural gift called "the gift of the discerning of spirits" (see 1 Corinthians 12:10). This gift enables you to discern spirits, including demonic spirits. With this gift in operation, you can discern spirits such as narcissism, pride, selfishness, self-idolatry, etc., that are possibly binding the individual. Invite the Holy Spirit to fill you and give you this gift. Usually you will receive your first alert concerning narcissism by observing behaviors, but the discerning of spirits will help to confirm if there are also spiritual forces involved.

When a doctor is searching for a root cause, he does not simply look at one or two symptoms to complete his diagnosis. It requires a fuller profile with a number of matching symptoms. As we study the list of symptoms below, you will usually identify many, but not all, in an individual who is struggling.

Jesus also taught us to examine ourselves first so that we can freely help others, so it will be advantageous to go through this list and examine yourself first. It is an enlightening exercise.

"And why do you look at the speck in your brother's eye, but do not consider the plank in your own eye? Or how can you say to your brother, 'Let me remove the speck from your eye'; and look, a plank is in your own eye? ... First remove the plank from your own eye, and then you will see clearly to remove the speck from your brother's eye." (Matthew 7:3-5)

Symptoms of Narcissism

Those who display narcissistic behavior will often manifest a number of the following symptoms:

1. Pride, arrogance, and entitlement.

2. Brag on their achievements.

3. Blame others for their shortcomings.

4. Focus on outward physical and material appearances.

5. Focus on an increase of material possessions; materialistic.

6. Look for associations that make them "look good" or who will benefit their agendas and progress.

7. Self-focused, self-absorbed, self-admiration, self-gratification, selfish ambition.

8. Poor listeners to others who are engaged in conversation with them.

9. Manipulate in order to achieve their plans and fulfill their agendas.

10. Motivated to engage in relationships only for self-gratification.

11. Look for attention, esteem and honor from others towards them.

12. Make decisions based on their personal benefit and not for the sake of others.

13. Exploit people, their gifts and sphere of influence, in order to advance their own selfish purposes and gain.

14. Will be kind and generous only if it ultimately benefits them.

15. Use charm to get their way – often very charismatic. Narcissists usually have a charisma about them that they employ either knowingly or not knowingly to attract the attention of others.

16. Are never fully satisfied.

17. Lack empathy.

18. Blinded to their shortcomings and are not usually willing to have others point out faults even if the confrontation is delivered in a loving way.

19. Celebrity mindset (love the limelight and special attention as a VIP).

20. Often have addictive and compulsive disorders.

21. Vanity.

22. Aggression and angry outbursts, especially when confronted or opposed.

23. Shallow values.

24. Prone to lies, exaggerations and fabrications.

25. Blame and shame shifts when confronted or convicted; lack of true conviction.

26. Do not care about the effect of their choices on others as long as it is beneficial for them.

27. Obsessed with fantasies of unlimited success.

28. Require excessive praise, admiration and adulation.

29. Demand immediate compliance to their orders, instructions, expectations and directions.

30. Feel grandiose – exaggerated sense of self-importance.

31. Listen to what others have to say only if it mirrors their own viewpoints.

32. Believe that the only great ideas are their own.

33. Underestimate challenges facing them and pretend to be a "know-it-all."

34. Appear to be overconfident.

35. Demand attention.

36. Cannot forget a wrong done to them and may be prone to seek revenge.

37. May have a condescending or belittling attitude toward their employees, employer or other relationships in their life.

38. Overrate their accomplishments – they have an inflated opinion of themselves.

39. Controlling – sometimes subtle as in passive-aggressive.

40. Spends money on self – often in debt.

41. Competitive – often compares their accomplishments, skills, and possessions to others.

42. Want to be the center of attention.

43. Abusive – emotional, spiritual, physical, and/or sexual.

44. Believe they are the exception to any rules that do not support their agenda.

45. Sexual misconduct, obsessions, and behavior.

To some, narcissists may seem like they have great confidence or high self-esteem. Unfortunately, those with narcissistic personality disorder cross the border of healthy confidence and self-esteem into thinking so highly of themselves that they put themselves on pedestals. People who have healthy confidence and self-esteem don't value themselves more than they value others. Jesus said that to be great in the Kingdom of God was to be least of all. A true heart of a servant is to lift up others, and God promises to lift us up if we do. We do not have to do our own lifting up!

Pride goes before destruction, and a haughty spirit before stumbling. (Proverbs 16:18)

Sitting down, He called the twelve and said to them, "If anyone wants to be first, he shall be last of all and servant of all." (Mark 9:35)

"Whoever then humbles himself as this child, he is the greatest in the kingdom of heaven." (Matthew 18:4)

THE FRUIT OF NARCISSISM

The following are some examples of possible fruit following those bound by narcissism:

1. Broken relationships and covenants

2. Division in homes, workplaces, spheres of influence, relationships, and church

3. Mental illness – breakdowns, depression, compulsive disorders, sociopathic behavior in severe cases

4. Criminal activity

5. Error and Deception – in their determination to "be right" and not submit to those who speak into their lives, they engage in deception.

6. Cults can form

7. Abuse

EXAMPLES OF NARCISSISTIC BEHAVIOR

Narcissism can be found anywhere – in the home, the workplace, in schools and, yes, even in the church. The following examples are scenarios that reveal narcissistic behavior in different environments.[1]

Brandon

Brandon, a 17-year-old, broke into his grandmother's home and stole her entire gold coin collection appraised at approximately

---

1 The examples used in this book do not include the real name of the one represented. Some are based on real stories and others are fictional, created, extracted, and edited from various sources.

$20,000. Immediately after the theft, he sold it at a pawn shop for less than $1,500 cash.

His parents and grandmother reported the crime when they discovered the coin collection missing. Eventually they were called to the local police station when the law enforcement officers arrested the thief. They were shocked, perplexed, shaken and deeply hurt to find that their own son and grandson, Brandon, had violated and betrayed them in this way. His mother, weeping uncontrollably, asked, "Why? Why? I can't believe that you stole from your own grandmother! Why?"

He unashamedly explained that he had overheard the family reviewing his grandmother's will as she was putting her estate in order. He was upset that his name was not included, so he decided he would take something for himself. He said, "She's not going to be around for many more years, and a few coins aren't going to make a difference." There was no remorse for what he did; rather he was upset that he was caught. His grandmother dropped all charges.

Through the process, the parents further discovered that Brandon was using drugs. When confronted, he simply explained that he was entitled to feel good. There was no repentance. He eventually was caught in another theft and was upset about being caught and demanded seasoned legal support to get him off the charges, as he did not feel he deserved the consequences that a judge might issue.

Although his family loved him, Brandon was self-absorbed and could not reciprocate that love. His world was all about him. A spirit of narcissism fueled Brandon's self-idolatrous behavior.

Megan

Megan was the only daughter and the youngest child in a family of four children. Her parents had wanted a girl from the time they were expecting their second child. Megan was born prematurely and at first they were not sure she would survive, so when she finally came home from the hospital after weeks of intensive care, she was the center of attention in the home.

The "princess" learned how to charm her parents and her brothers at an early age. She received a great deal of affirmation and attention in the home. She could do no wrong in the eyes of her family, and the sun rose and set upon her. As a result, she became very self-focused and absorbed. Some days she would change her clothes several times in order to hear her family tell her how great she looked. She loved the attention, and if they were not giving it to her, she would find a way to get it.

When Megan went to school she hit a crisis. She discovered quickly that in the schoolyard she was not the center of attention like she was in her home. This was the beginning of discovering and activating deceptive, attention-getting behavior. She placed demands on her parents for new clothes because she found that when she donned a new, trendy outfit at school, she received extra attention from the other girls coveting her apparel. She liked being envied. She was obsessed with her appearance by the fifth grade, and often stood in front of a mirror for long periods of time admiring herself. She bought glamour magazines by the rack and determined to keep up with the latest fashions.

She started to physically develop as a woman in the seventh grade and became obsessed with the attention of boys. She made sure she acquired their admiration and learned seductive ways to attract them. From adolescence, she loved the attention of the opposite sex but never wanted to commit to any. All of her romantic relationships were short-lived, as they failed to meet and fulfill her needs. She would abruptly terminate one and go to the next. She was rejected by the girls at school but did not seem to mind that as she felt superior to them.

When she turned 16, she asked her parents for breast implant surgery for her birthday present. They discouraged her but promised that if she still wanted the surgery at age 21, they would give it to her as a special birthday present – which she did. In fact, by the time she was 25, she had already gone through numerous cosmetic surgeries, treatments and, yes, the breast implant. She was also obsessed with diet and exercise, and suffered from a shopping addiction. Megan was enamored with her appearance. She lived to hear the approval of others. She lived to be the center of attention.

Megan became competitive and successful in her career as a salesperson for a cosmetic company. She learned to aggressively pursue business connections that would further her career. She was not genuinely interested in meeting her clients, but made it appear that way so she could get what she wanted from them. She built convenient business connections in order to climb the corporate ladder and did not care about stepping on anyone's toes to get what she wanted. Every choice in life was about what benefited her personally.

One evening she was watching a television feature on a particular Hollywood celebrity whom she admired. The feature highlighted the generosity of the actress and boasted on her compassionate and giving heart. The program host interviewed young admirers of this actress who were deeply touched by this aspect of her character. One girl cried out as the camera filmed her, "She has so much love!" She then hysterically screamed idolatrous accolades into the camera.

The very next day after viewing the program, Megan made a large contribution to a charity and let everyone know about it. She privately admitted to some friends that she did not have a heart for the needy at all but the public, ostentatious, display of her generosity gave her favor with some influential people in her field. She was using her fabricated act of benevolence for personal leverage. Her motive in publicly demonstrating generosity was to receive attention and personal benefit from her good works. If the benevolent deed did not give opportunity for personal gratification, then she would not have done it. Later she openly and shamelessly admitted to this.

She got married when she was 29, but divorced her husband within 18 months because, due to company downsizing, he was demoted in his job, with less pay, and no longer had the means to treat her as she felt she deserved.

A spirit of narcissism possessed Megan.

Brian

Brian grew up in a very dysfunctional home. Every day there were fights between his parents. Anger and rage were the order of the day in his household. Both his parents were addicted to drugs and alcohol. His father would leave the home for months at a time. When Brian was five years old, his father left for good. His mother neglected him due to her addictions, and he was eventually removed from his home and placed in foster care.

Brian got involved with a group of rebels in school and entered a life of crime and addiction at an early age. He was sentenced to juvenile detention for the first time at age 14 and was in and out of detention over the next number of years due to his developing life of crime. While institutionalized, he learned to become a master liar and manipulator.

31

Years later he openly admitted to the skillful lies he regularly communicated, and he boasted to many about how he had learned to get his way with any guard or counselor in the system.

At age 21 he had a genuine spiritual encounter that transformed his life. He enjoyed true love and care for the first time in his existence. Jesus Christ powerfully entered his life. Brian experienced God-given, supernatural visitations following his conversion, and he joined a local church. He was mentored as a new believer by a pastor who truly cared for him. Shortly after, he married a lovely young lady he met in church. They had a family together and he delighted in his new life in Christ, saying that he had never been happier.

Five years into their marriage, he planted a church. His congregation honored and exalted him as a mighty man of God. His church quickly grew and he expanded his ministry to local television. Young women in the church started showing him attention and affection. Congregation members often gave him extravagant personal gifts, business and vacation opportunities, as well as generous amounts of money. He aligned himself with business owners and city government leaders, befriending them in order to obtain their favor and public endorsement for his increasing sphere of influence. Within the first three years of his initial church plant, he had greatly expanded. The church continued to grow and expand their reach over the next five years.

Over time, the growing demands of his church and ministry took a toll on his marriage, and he decided that he deserved better. Why should he live in an uncomfortable marriage when he had lost his fresh love for his wife and "the cream of the crop" was readily available to him? Many women were enamored with his anointing and charisma. Why should he give his wife the time of day when she was not 100% in support of his ministry anyway? Why should he care about her when she was not giving him what he needed or wanted? Why should he put up with that kind of tension in his life?

Brian's children were his public trophies. They were intelligent, well-behaved, attractive and well-groomed. He introduced his wife and children every Sunday morning in church, having them stand, smile, and greet church members. He would honor them in public in order to impress the congregation by painting the picture of the model family, but it was all for show. Behind the scenes he emotionally abused and neglected both his wife and his children.

Everything in Brian's life was about him. He lied, flirted with young women in the church, watched pornography on the Internet, went on drinking sprees and frequently spent church money inappropriately on personal pleasures. He openly preached against such things but privately considered himself an exception to the rule. He loved his ministry and the attention it gave him. He put "yes men" around himself and operated in control and manipulation to achieve his agendas. His anointing and the ministry of the Spirit and the Word were authentic, but his motives in ministry and his personal life were about fulfilling his own pleasures. His character and behaviors violated biblical values and standards for believers and especially for leaders.

His son was 12 and his daughter 10 when Brian was publicly exposed for having a sexual affair with a beautiful young woman who worked as his personal assistant. The media had a heyday exposing his antics and hypocrisy. His family and the church were devastated. Although he was caught, there was no true remorse, only feigned. Before the public he shed remorseful tears and appeared humbled and broken, but behind the scenes he justified his actions, saying that his wife was falling short of giving him what he needed. Nothing in his world was ever truly his fault. He shared privately with his church board that his wife would often lose her temper, swear at him and had thrown objects at him while in a rage. He concluded, "No man of God needs to put up with this. I deserve better and I am going to have better. Any man in my situation would have done the same thing." They tried to convince him to work out the problems in his marriage and to think of his children, but he refused. He emphatically stated, "I have been miserable in this marriage for a few years already and now it is time for me to be happy. I deserve it."

When they questioned his wife, they learned she had suffered years of emotional abuse and neglect. She admitted to regretfully losing her temper and with hesitation confessed that she felt harassed, pressured and controlled to a point where she would "lose it."

The church board made him step down from his pastorate due to his moral failure, his lack of true repentance, and his refusal to walk through normal restoration processes. He was very angry with them and took them to court, demanding a large severance. He won the court battle and received a generous settlement in his favor. He filed for divorce from his wife. Although she contested the divorce and wanted to work things out, he was awarded it. He gave her custody of their children with visitation privileges and agreed to pay the minimum support required by law for the maintenance of his wife and children.

Brian moved to a different state to start his new life. He had pushed his divorce through quickly, and the moment it was official he eloped with his lover. He bought himself and his new wife a new home, with all the furnishings, from his severance and the court settlement.

He often failed to pay the alimony and child support in full and seldom called or visited his children. When he did, he spent large amounts of money on them, lavished them with gifts, and told them how much he loved them. He often publicly testified of how much he loved his children and how much he blessed them.

His family and his local church were shipwrecked. In the midst of it, Brian boasted to personal friends that he had never been happier. One concerned board member said to him, "Don't you care about all the people you have hurt?" He responded, "Yeah, but they will get over it. They have to forgive me. I'm hurting, too, because of the way they have treated me." It was all about Brian.

Brian used his charisma, faith and magnetic personality to build another congregation within a year of his divorce and remarriage. After four years, Brian was once again disillusioned with his wife and the confinements that their new baby brought to his ministry and life. The old patterns were in full motion again.

A spirit of narcissism deceived Brian.

Allison

Allison was a beautiful 32-year-old single woman and a successful executive in an advertising firm. She had won numerous awards for her performance in the company and she had become close to Doug, the company's CEO. Doug was 48 years old and had been happily married to his wife for 22 years. He had two college-aged children who were the pride of his life. He would often talk about his wife and children. His office was full of framed photos and he was a good family man, successful in all his endeavors.

Allison envied his wife and was eaten up with desire to have Doug for herself. She would sometimes by the hour imagine schemes to capture his heart, and she made it her goal to become "his woman." This was not the first time Allison had ruined a marriage. She pursued married men. They began to go out for meals after work and labor together on projects alone. Eventually her seductions and manipulations drew his heart and an emotional affair developed between them.

Doug was often confused and wavered back and forth, determining to pull out of the relationship, but Allison would always convince him that they were made for each other. One weekend while attending a convention in another city, Allison invited him to her hotel room to talk over some business strategies. After having a few drinks they tragically ended up in a sexual relationship.

Doug came to the realization of what he had done and felt deep remorse. He attempted to cut off the relationship once and for all, but Allison manipulated him more with dramatic emotional outbursts and threats. He didn't want to hurt her, so he continued in the relationship for a season until he was completely overcome with guilt and shame. He finally confessed to his wife and ended the affair. His wife was wounded beyond belief but she forgave him. They went to marriage counseling and started to rebuild the broken foundations.

Doug asked Allison to leave the company in light of the situation. When she resisted, he fired her due to some other complaints that had been brought forward by co-workers. She was very angry and not willing to let go of her position. She did not care that she had deeply hurt Doug, his wife, his family and the workplace. She did not care that she had harmed a marriage. She began to spread terrible rumors and lies about him to those in the company which resulted in gossip, dishonor, and division within the company. She was only concerned about herself and was very irate about her loss. One of her co-workers challenged her one day regarding her attitude and behaviors. She responded, "But what about me? I have been hurt in this, too. He dumped me! How do you think I feel?" No one could convince her that she had done wrong. According to her perspective, she was the victim.

Allison finally did leave the company and moved on, but not without a fight. She went to human resources and then secured an attorney. At the end of the process she sued Doug and the company and won a settlement. She told a friend after the court awarded her the settlement, "What I received is nothing compared to what I would have gotten if he had married me. The guy is worth millions and I would have lived in luxury for life. He should have left his wife and married me. His wife is not worthy of him."

The spirit of narcissism controlled Allison.

Gordon

Gordon worked at a high-end department store as a salesman in the shoe department. He had a base income with performance bonuses. Gordon was highly successful in sales but was unscrupulous in his tactics. He was uncaring about the effects of the manipulations and pressures he made on the clients or other salespersons in his department. Although committed to prosperity in sales, he ambitiously desired the management position, which he eventually was awarded. As a manager, Gordon failed terribly. His narcissistic agendas were obvious to the sales staff and they were not motivated to perform for him. He took all the credit for their sales and rudely pressured them when their performance was not up to his expectations. He also pressured customers when they walked away without making a purchase. Many quit his department. He was brought before the store manager and confronted concerning his shortcomings. Gordon became very defensive and went into a rage. He blamed his staff and put demands on the store manager for more income and better staff. His selfish attitude, numerous demands, blame shifting and lack of restraint contributed to his immediate termination. Gordon was fired that day due to numerous filed complaints against him both by customers and his sales team.

Gordon was angry when he went home that evening to his wife of four years. His wife was a hard-working teacher at the local elementary school. She was a faithful wife and tried to comfort him, but he refused comfort. He was up all night pacing back and forth, rehearsing retaliation. He finally wrote his overseer an email full of anger and demanded that he meet with him. His request was denied by the company's corporate management later the next day. Gordon did not sleep at all that night. When his wife woke up, he once again dumped on her with his angry perspective.

Later that morning, after his wife went to work, he looked through the newspaper and noticed a seminar on business success in the classified ads. He signed up for it, hoping that it might open doors for him. He needed something big to open up fast, as he had no savings. He always spent his money on his personal wardrobe, grooming, new vehicles and on the latest and greatest entertainment media.

At the business seminar, Gordon was very impressed with the presenter. He liked the vibrant dynamics he moved in, his trendy appearance, excellent physique, and was especially impacted by the testimony of his multi-million dollar business success. Throughout the seminar he envisioned himself in the presenter's shoes. He purchased the $2,500 success motivation training DVDs with his wife's credit card. He immediately went into his home office, locked the door and began watching the DVDs by the hour. When his wife asked him to come out and join her for dinner, he opened the door with his eyes glazed over and said, "Do not disturb me. I am going to be a very successful businessman making millions of dollars every year." He locked himself in the room day after day, preparing for the millions. After a week or two, he informed his wife that he was going to start a business, but he needed her financial help. She explained to him that she already needed to make extra money to pay off the $2,500 expense for the DVDs, as well as all the household bills that he was no longer contributing towards. He convinced her to sign for a loan for his business startup. He informed her that he was going to teach success motivation seminars and make thousands of dollars every week. He also informed her that he was going to create a product with his teachings (that were based on what he learned through the DVDs) as well as film an infomercial where he could make millions by selling the product and advertising his seminars.

His wife was completely opposed to his business plan and explained that he did not have enough experience and success in business to be able to teach it yet. He glared at her with his finger pointed in her face, saying, "Don't you ever question my ability to perform. I am called to do this and I will do it. I am going to apply for a $150,000 line of credit on the house and you WILL sign for it. You will not hold me back!"

Through pressure, his wife consented to sign for the line of credit. He sold his car and bought a higher end one, and spent $15,000 on a new wardrobe. He paid a graphic designer to brand his new endeavor, paid for advertising and marketing, rented a hotel conference room and hired a producer for the infomercial. He quickly absorbed the $150,000 and also maxed out their credit cards.

Every aspect of his plan was an absolute flop. His inexperience was obvious to *all three* participants in his first seminar, and to the producer/director of the infomercial. He was offended with the instructions of the director and fired him halfway through, deciding to direct himself, telling the camera personnel what to do in order to get the best shot of him.

When he pitched his infomercial to television stations, they were appalled at the "cheesiness" of the production, and he received one rejection letter after another. He was finally accepted by an obscure station in a small region of the USA that was willing to broadcast him at 3 a.m. at a budget rate of thousands per hour. He had the misconception that stations would pay him to air the program. He had no budget left for airtime and was left at a standstill.

Gordon would not admit to his mistakes and tension increased in the marriage. He made demands on his wife to work extra jobs in order to support the household needs and his debt. He hid himself in his study, watching videos of successful businessmen, and he watched infomercials on television networks, dreaming of the day when he would make his millions.

His wife invited a pastor over to speak into Gordon's life, but it only made him angry. After the pastor left, he yelled at his wife, accusing her of not supporting him. Gordon continued to emotionally abuse her. One night he came home after watching a movie and found a note from his wife saying she couldn't take it any longer and had decided to leave him. Gordon was angry and wanted sympathy, but few of their friends would agree with him. Many pleaded with him to get some help, but he refused. He blamed his wife for his failure. He blamed the church for not supporting his choices. He pointed his finger at everyone but himself.

Over the next three years, his wife returned twice to give the marriage another try. Each time she was met with more abuse. She finally left for good and moved to another part of the country to start a new life. Gordon put so much emotional pressure on her that she made a decision to take nothing with her. All their furniture and belongings were left with Gordon. He lost the house when the bank repossessed it for lack of payments, and yet he blamed the economy. After losing the house, he sold all the furniture and even lived in the back of his car for a short period. Gordon was alone. No one could speak sense into him. He was unteachable, unreachable.

A spirit of narcissism blinded and controlled Gordon.

Wallace

Wallace was a filmmaker who climbed up through the ranks. Narcissistic behaviors manifested in his life from an early age. As a young man he was very ambitious and had the goal to reach the top of the industry at any cost – and in time, he did.

His climb to the top involved layers of manipulation and control. He would form partnerships along the way that would advance his goals, and then find legal loopholes in the contracts to disqualify his partners, often taking ownership of their shares and leaving them bankrupt. He felt no remorse, only a feeling of entitlement, and he celebrated his courtroom wins with massive parties. This happened several times. He rallied a team around him who idolized him. They were at his beck and call. He overworked his staff and quickly replaced anyone who resisted him. They were all called to sign confidentiality agreements and other documents that would keep them from reporting any shady behaviors they noticed "in-house."

He gave himself to self-sexual fulfillment and was sexually inappropriate with many of the women who worked for him. One girl, named Shelly, was invited into his office at his request during the first week she was hired. She felt honored to be asked by him to meet him face-to-face, as he was very well known and extremely influential. Shelly desired to grow in the entertainment industry as a producer and was willing to work in humble positions to get her foot in the door.

When she approached his office, the secretary announced her to Wallace and ushered her into his "palace." Shelly sat across from his desk and was starstruck as he showed an interest in her, asking questions about her life, her desires for filmmaking, and her family. He then stood up from behind his desk and moved toward her. He stood behind her and began to massage her shoulders as he continued to ask questions and initiate a conversation. She became very uncomfortable but did not know what to do. After all, this was "Wallace." His hands then moved from the shoulders down under her blouse and touched her breasts. She pulled his hands off her and jumped up out of her seat, stating emphatically that she was not open to that. He moved toward her and said, "If you are going to work here, you will give me what I ask, when I ask." She moved away from him but he continued to follow her. He then started to unzip his pants. She raised her voice, but he continued to come after her. She went towards the door to exit the office, but it was difficult to open. She pounded on it, hoping the secretary would open it. He threatened her, saying that if she did not comply, she would have every door of opportunity closed to her in the industry...that he would make sure that happened. He said, "Believe me, you do not want to be my enemy." He was pressing himself behind her as she continued to try to leave.

Shelly finally was able to open the door, and left the office disheveled, noticing the secretary. It appeared that she had seen this scenario before and just continued on working as if nothing had happened. That day Shelly resigned her position without notice and was greatly disillusioned. Just as Wallace had threatened, other doors of opportunity had been closed to her.

Many years later, a few women who had been treated in similar ways, and even allegedly raped, reported him. In addition to his legal team, he gathered a group of people around him to support him – many of them paid off with favors, as he attempted to make it all go away – but the women courageously held their ground. The media became aware, and exposure of his treatment of the women was splashed all over the nation. More and more women came forward. He had violated hundreds over the years. It finally went to trial. He was without remorse and believed he would get off. He arrogantly built a narrative, denying the allegations and blaming the women for wanting his money and his influence. His team around him supported him, as many were afraid not to and others were deceived into believing him.

No remorse. No repentance. Wallace was bound by narcissism.

NARCISSISM IN THE CHURCH

There are many wonderful, humble, and self-sacrificing leaders in the body of Christ. They are true servants who love the Lord and minister to His people with grace and humility. Most of the leaders I know are definitely of that heart and posture. However, the spirit of narcissism can tempt and control those in the body who are ignorant of the enemy's devices and who do not guard their hearts. And leaders can be susceptible to this spirit due to the celebrity treatment that is expected and demanded by some.

Ministers who are bound by narcissism are often very charismatic leaders who have magnetic personalities. They love the limelight and demand special attention, including monetary extravagance, often in the name of "honor." They may have grown up in a troubled, abusive or neglected home life or childhood. Through ignorance or pride they may not have allowed the Holy Spirit the freedom to heal them completely. Unteachable, unreachable and prideful, the narcissistic leader can confuse, numb and deceive others into thinking they are invincible, anointed, powerful, and deserving of "superstar" treatment. Those who work for them or who follow them are often deceived and controlled by deceptive mindsets and teachings that fortify the leader's self-idolatry. In extreme cases, you find examples such as cult leader Jim Jones, who in 1978 led over 900 of his followers to their death through a mass suicide.

Unresolved narcissistic behaviors in a leader can have a variety of effects on his/her followers or congregation. This leader mentors and clones other leaders who "mirror" the leader's self-centered personality and deception. The narcissist patterns are both taught and "caught," and thus transferred to others.

Evangelist Tramel

Evangelist Tramel was an anointed preacher and his charismatic personality quickly won the hearts of those he ministered to. Miracles were commonplace in his ministry and he was very accurate in the prophetic gift[2] and words of knowledge[3].

---

2 Prophecy is one of the nine gifts of the Spirit mentioned in 1 Corinthians 12:4-11. It is the ability to foretell future events and to proclaim words of destiny over people's lives, regions and nations.

3 Word of knowledge is one of the nine gifts of the Spirit mentioned in 1 Corinthians 12:4-11. This gift enables a believer to know things about a person or a situation through supernatural means.

His ministry grew to a place where he was hosting crowds of thousands, and he gained much media attention. He became very entitled, arrogant, and focused on the favor he was receiving, in addition to being preoccupied with the large amount of money that was being raised in his meetings. He would constantly mention from the pulpit about "his ministry" and how anointed he was. Behind the scenes, he demanded special treatment and bragged about his ministry "performance" and about the money he was making.

He had an internship program to train others in the ministry of soul winning and signs and wonders. The interns were taught that as a minister they were to demand respect, and when they went to preach in a church, they were to be well looked after and to use the churches to gain a following. He trained them to expect generous remuneration for their services and if it wasn't enough, to ask for more.

Not only was Evangelist Tramel clearly narcissistic in behavior, but he also taught those behaviors to the others who worked with him. You become like the company you keep, and if your leader is a narcissist, you could fall prey. When you walk in pride, eventually you will fall and, unfortunately, you will take others with you. It has a domino effect. "Pride comes before the fall" (see Proverbs 16:18). The following proverb is interesting in light of this:

If a ruler pays attention to falsehood, all his ministers become wicked. (Proverbs 29:12)

In consideration of this scriptural insight, over time, if an unrepentant narcissistic leader continues to oversee you in the church or ministry, I would highly recommend leaving in honor, no matter what benefits you might receive from their gifts and anointing.

WHEN NARCISSISM EVOLVES INTO ABUSE

As mentioned before, there are many wonderful, humble and self-sacrificing leaders in the body of Christ. These include highly successful visionary leaders who must count on a dedicated team to help carry out their God-given vision. Understandably, they require team members who are hard-working, willing to work behind-the-scenes, loyal, and also wholeheartedly embrace the vision. The leader, on the other hand, genuinely cares for the team members and their wellbeing. They do not consider themselves "superior" to those they serve; rather, they exemplify Christ. Jesus' itinerary was extremely demanding, but He constantly modeled genuine leadership/servant-hood to His disciples (John 17). He rejoiced in watching them grow into the roles He was preparing them for.

On the other hand, a leader bound by a spirit of narcissism, if unrestrained, may eventually evolve into the following extremes.

This leader:

1. Becomes emotionally abusive in order to establish superiority; e.g., speaks and treats others in a demeaning way, constantly reminding them of their "lowly status" and that they are only there to serve their leader, no matter what; ridicules and humiliates others both publicly and privately, uses fear and intimidation, etc.

2. States that "they" are God's chosen ministry for the hour and anyone who questions anything they are teaching/do-ing – no matter how respectfully – or chooses to leave said ministry, is under deception, out of God's will, "in rebellion" and often deemed "persona non grata."

3. Has no concern for their team members' well-being, safety or this person's other relationships; they only care about themselves.

The line has crossed into moral degradation when a leader demands or manipulates someone to break established laws – man or God's – including shady finances and sexual immorality. We hear more and more of innocent victims who became the prey of the immoral sexual appetites of manipulative leaders. No matter how "anointed" a leader is, God gives no one a "pass" to sin. They are just as accountable to God as the next person and, eventually, will pay the price. King David learned this the hard way.

If you, or someone you are aware of, has become a victim of a leader's physical or sexual abuse, it is vital that it be reported to someone in authority. If another leader in their own ministry doesn't consider it an issue, or even tries to silence you, then go to someone else you trust, until someone listens and takes action. In cases of minor abuse or rape, always go to the civil authorities, not only for justice but also so that others will be protected from future abuse. Never be too ashamed, fearful, or intimidated to do so – you are precious to the Lord.

A leader who is bound by this spirit needs rescue – and so do their followers. We must be discerning, alert, and sensitive to the Holy Spirit. Our discernment must never cross a line and turn to bitter judgment and criticism. Unconditional love that knows healthy boundaries and makes wise decisions will motivate you to embrace the power of life-changing, fervent and relentless prayer that can work glorious miracles of freedom. There is always hope, even if you need to pray from afar.

I urge, then, first of all, that requests, prayers, intercession and thanksgiving be made for everyone – for kings and all those in authority, that we may live peaceful and quiet lives in all godliness and holiness. This is good, and pleases God our Savior, who wants all men to be saved and to come to a knowledge of the truth (1 Timothy 2:1-4 NIV).

Questions to Ponder

1. How do the media – and the church – celebrate, and even encourage, narcissistic behavior?

2. Read through the symptoms again and consider what the "opposite" (Christlike) spirit would look like in each case.

3. Have you ever been under, or influenced by, a leader who was narcissistic? How did it affect your perceptions regarding Jesus, the church, yourself, and others? What steps did you take to distance yourself? If this is a present circumstance, do you feel motivated to do something at this point?

4. What would "leaving with honor" look like?

5. Think of one to three takeaways from this chapter. Why were these highlighted to you? How did they influence or change your thinking? Are there any actions you need to take based on these?

6. Have you been wounded by a narcissistic authority (family, civil, career-related, spiritual, etc.)? Have you experienced healing? Write a prayer of forgiveness (and also ask for the grace to forgive), and intercession – that this person may be released from deception and be transformed. Seek help if you are still struggling (chapter 4 will also give further insight).

CHAPTER THREE

OVERCOMING NARCISSISM

Whether you suffer with the actual disorder, a demonic bondage, or even light symptoms of narcissistic behavior – narcissism can be overcome! If you have a desire to be free, you can be. All things are possible, only believe. "So if the Son makes you free, you will be free indeed" (John 8:36). "You will know the truth, and the truth will make you free" (John 8:32). Jesus Himself is the truth who will set you free, and His Word gives clear instruction on how to overcome narcissism.

ADMIT YOU NEED HELP – HONEST EVALUATION

Until an individual recognizes their need for help, they will not be able to get free. The Holy Spirit convicts of sin, but because of the nature of the deception involved in narcissistic behavior and the hardening of heart that occurs, an intervention is almost always needed. Depending on the degree of deception, in an intervention, concerned family members, friends or co-workers will sit down and lovingly and skillfully confront their specific concerns identifying the narcissistic patterns. The persons involved in intervention must have genuine, deep care for the narcissist. They also need the maturity to establish boundaries and to resist the rejection, blame and retaliation that will most likely be directed at them at some point during or following the intervention. They must be discerning and able to withstand manipulation. Getting a narcissist to see their need for help is absolutely essential to freedom. It is a challenging assignment and needs much prayer, but all things are possible.

> But He gives a greater grace. Therefore it says, "God is opposed
> to the proud, but gives grace to the humble." (James 4:6)

TRUE, HEARTFELT REPENTANCE

The narcissist must take ownership for their actions and motivations, and be willing to sincerely repent. Repentance is not merely saying sorry but rather, it involves taking full ownership and responsibility for a wrong and a true turning away from it. Someone bound by this disorder must confess their sins associated with narcissism, repent, and receive forgiveness. True repentance is the foundation for freedom.

Narcissism hurts others. It is important for a narcissist to seriously take ownership of how they have hurt others. Making a list of the people they have hurt and the ways they have hurt them is highly beneficial. The Holy Spirit is able to bring things to their mind. After the list is complete, they should ask the Lord to forgive them, and they need to also ask for forgiveness from those they have hurt. It may also be necessary to make restitution.

An individual bound by narcissism is deceived and therefore they cannot see the areas they need to repent of until revelation comes. Neither will they understand how they have hurt others or why they need to make things right with them. Due to these dynamics and in order for freedom to come, they will need those they choose to trust to speak clear, uncompromised truth to them and to hold them accountable.

The tendency of a narcissist is to repent for as little as possible, although initially even that might not be truly heartfelt. They will oftentimes admit to a measure of sin and verbally say they are taking responsibility, only to keep the pressure off so exposure will not come to the deeper issues – similar to an iceberg effect. When you see an iceberg in the sea, you are only seeing a small tip in comparison to what lies beneath. Those who help a narcissist come to the truth might need to dig deeper with them in order for them to bring full disclosure.

Without full disclosure and true repentance, freedom cannot come.

DIE TO SELF

Jesus taught us to deny ourselves, take up our cross daily and follow Him (see Luke 9:23).

If you are bound by narcissism, **there is only one way to receive complete deliverance and that is to die – "die to self."** In the myth, Narcissus was unable to overcome – no matter who tried to bring comfort or consolation. He finally died at the side of the pond. In that place of death, a beautiful flower came forth.

Jesus offers us freedom through His death on the cross. We are taught in Scripture to reckon ourselves dead to sin. We are to see ourselves "crucified with Christ" as we identify with His death. We cannot experience resurrection into the new life of Christ until we embrace death to self. The cross came before resurrection. The sins of selfishness, self-absorption, self-exaltation and self-focus can all be dealt with through the power of the cross. They were nailed to the cross in Christ two thousand years ago. The cross is an instrument of death.

When we die to ourselves, we are then free to live to serve others and to love others. A dead person is unable to act selfishly, get offended, or walk in pride. We are to reckon ourselves dead to sin and alive to God. Like Jesus, we choose to deny ourselves and live for the benefit of others. "Unless a grain of wheat falls into the earth and dies, it remains alone; but if it dies, it bears much fruit" (John 12:24). In the myth, the beautiful flower did not come forth until Narcissus died.

Those who are free from narcissism look for ways they can serve and empower others. Their motives are pure and are not tied to the reward they will receive back from it. They are free to serve others well and always esteem others higher than themselves. Selfish ambition has been nailed to the cross, and loving servanthood is the motivation of their actions of service.

> But he that is greatest among you shall be your servant. And whosoever shall exalt himself shall be abased; and he that shall humble himself shall be exalted. (Matthew 23:11-12 KJV)

DEAL WITH THE ROOTS

Where there is bad fruit, there is a bad root. The root(s) need to be identified and dealt with.

> "The axe is already laid at the root of the trees; therefore every tree that does not bear good fruit is cut down and thrown into the fire." (Matthew 3:10)

1. Generational iniquity. The Bible states that the sins of the parents are visited on the children to the third and fourth generations (see Exodus 20:5). It is possible for sins associated with narcissism, such as self-centeredness, self-idolatry and pride, to be passed down through the generational line in the same way physical weaknesses are sometimes passed down from one generation to another. Deliverance from narcissism can be experienced when we identify generational roots, forgive our forefathers, and by faith cut off the generational transference.[4]

2. Childhood rejection, abuse and/or neglect. The onset of narcissism is usually in infancy, childhood, and early adolescence. The first five years of a child's life are extremely important in their emotional and behavioral development. If a child is rejected, neglected, or emotionally, verbally, physically or sexually abused, the effects of it could create an established foundation of brokenness in the inner heart. That broken, bruised and empty place longs to be whole. We were not created to be rejected or mistreated, but loved and accepted. When true love and acceptance are not shown to a child, then vulnerability to responses such as self-focus and self-absorption can set them up for narcissistic patterns. A child does not know how to rightly discern these issues. They just know they feel empty and bad inside and want to feel good. This empty, rejected, neglected or abused place within is a landing strip for narcissism. That place in their heart will always demand to be satisfied with things that will make them feel good.

---

4 The transference of the attitudes and behavior can be transmitted from a narcissist to others through: (1) generational iniquitous strongholds; (2) taught behavior through official teaching of mindsets (i.e., a sales manager teaching his sales staff selfish motivational strategies); (3) living in the environment of narcissistic attitudes and "catching" the behavior.

A strict, legalistic religious upbringing can also produce narcissistic characteristic, as it is based on performance pressures and lacks true love and acceptance. Oftentimes in a religious setting, an individual will receive attention for their behaviors (good or bad), but it lacks the feeling of true nurture. The value is based on performance and accomplishments. This produces a vulnerability that can manifest in pride and/or a need for attention. The fear of lack of acceptance or rejection is what empowers narcissism through religious atmospheres.

Identifying the wounds of childhood rejection, neglect and abuse are an important part of freedom. Once they are identified, the one bound by narcissism can forgive those who hurt them, receive healing for the wounds, and break off the spiritual assignments of the enemy. Many books and courses are available that teach on the subject of healing childhood wounds and the process of inner healing.

Caleb

Oftentimes, narcissistic behaviors begin to develop in early childhood and are triggered by abandonment, abuse, or rejection. A young boy named Caleb was a "child genius." He had a very high IQ and was nicknamed "The Whiz Kid." Even as a toddler, his brilliant mind was easy to observe.

His father left the family when Caleb was only four, and the abandonment and rejection by his father was emotionally traumatic for Caleb. His mother had to work after the marriage breakup and Caleb was left with caregivers. At the time of their parent's separation, his older siblings were engaged in activities with their friends and were seldom available to spend time with Caleb. He felt very alone and afraid.

As a result he buried himself in books by the hour. He was able to read adult level academic books before he turned six. From a young age, both his parents entered him into many contests, competitions, and forums, and he even appeared on some television programs. He won every contest and tournament, and he gained attention from his father who attended all his competitions. By the time he was twelve, his home was filled with trophies and certificates, and he was granted many cash prizes and scholarships. His self-worth and value was built on the acceptance and honor he received from his accomplishments.

His family, friends and tutors treated him like a celebrity from a young age. He became the central focus for the family, and life revolved around his gift. His name and photograph were on posters, websites, and announcement media. Over time, he expected to be the center of attention and became extremely entitled. He grew up with a self-centered attitude. Whatever he demanded, he got. His every wish was his parents' command and he would play one against the other. He started manifesting narcissistic behavior from a young age and, unfortunately, he never grew out of it.

When he was 17, he had a psychotic episode, and his world collapsed around him. He was arrested and hospitalized due to some disturbing public behavior and, as a result, was medicated and diagnosed with a mental illness. He was treated for the disorder, but never fully recovered. He could no longer concentrate on his academics, and his mind lacked sharpness due to the medication. He was filled with hopelessness. The focus was still on him, but it was the kind of attention he did not want. The town's people were aware of what happened and there were whisperings everywhere – even a write-up in the local paper. The article was compassionate, sharing how he had been hospitalized for the health challenge, but the headline was cruel. His father and many other family members and friends had withdrawn from him after the initial crisis, not knowing how to cope with his mental illness. He was devastated and lost hope. Caleb never recovered, and he took his own life at age 21.

Note that Caleb carried a deep wound within his soul due to his father's abandonment back when he was only four. The deep-rooted fears of rejection that were birthed in that season set him up as a target for the spirit of narcissism. He was looking for something to fill the emptiness and void. He was looking for the security of love. All the attention he was given fed his longings, but it was only temporary. The void continued to cry out for more and more and was never quenched. It was never enough.

Good godly counseling, inner healing, and deliverance are important processes in healing these childhood wounds. Left unhealed, the individual becomes vulnerable to a spirit of narcissism.

3. Taught behavior patterns. If a person lives in an atmosphere of narcissistic behavior, they can easily learn to respond in like manner through constant example. Living or working in a narcissistic environment can be a setup for transference.

Ingrid

Ingrid grew up in a home where her parents were very focused and aggressive in their business. She often observed her parents compromise the well-being of others in order to establish advantages for themselves. They would boast about their antics openly with their children and teach them things like, "If you are going to be successful, then you have to do what you have to do. The strong one wins!" Her parents mocked the people they took advantage of in front of their children. Ingrid remembers her father saying, "They were idiots to fall for that plan. How stupid can you get? They deserve to lose their investment!"…Then he laughed.

They would take their earnings and buy better cars and furniture, take the children on exotic vacations and always boast in the fact that they "deserved the high life." They would also compare themselves with others in front of the children, saying things like, "Our family is much more successful than everyone else living on this block!" Ingrid grew up in an environment of narcissism and learned to do whatever it took to make herself happy and successful. She learned to manipulate, take advantage of, deceive, and seduce, in order to get her way. She learned the behavior.

When an adverse behavior is learned, it is important to recognize it, repent, get into healthy environments and relationships, and learn new patterns. This takes time to establish.

4. Celebrity treatment. When someone is constantly exalted and treated preferentially, they can come to believe that the world revolves around them. This is especially prevalent in our modern day social media. Individuals from a very young age can attract large followings due to their talent, gifting, or personality.

The "Man of God"

A minister once shared how they were taught in Bible school to keep a distance between themselves and the congregation. They were also taught that as a leader of the church they were "The Man of God" and deserved the double honor of the congregation. Of course, believers are to honor those who serve in leadership, but this situation got out of hand. He became an object of worship in his congregation. People were taught to give extravagant financial gifts to "The Man of God" in order to honor him, and were shunned if they didn't. He had a security squad around him to keep people from getting close. The church hired a chauffeur, personal tailor and chef for him. He treated all who worked for him with a condescending attitude and expected them to work for a low income as a holy sacrifice. He taught them that it was a divine blessing for them to serve "God's anointed servant." He, on the other hand, demanded an excessively large salary, with perks! After all, he was "The Man of God." His belief was that everyone existed in his life to bless him, "The Mighty Man of Faith." He had a very high opinion of himself. He was a gifted leader but he demanded celebrity treatment from those who were in his realm of influence. This VIP treatment and expectation became the root of his narcissistic behavior.

After a family tragedy, a nasty division in the church, and a major investment collapse, he sought counsel and discovered the patterns of narcissism that had formed as a result of his church "culture." He was greatly humbled through this series of tragic events, and through much ministry, inner healing, study, and therapy, he moved toward freedom from the deceptive mindsets of narcissism.

FOLLOW JESUS

Jesus sets such an amazing example for us. Oh, to be like Him! When we follow His ways, His words and His examples, there will be *no room left* for narcissistic behavior. The old hymn states, "I have decided to follow Jesus, no turning back, no turning back." Turning to Jesus completely, with a whole heart and following His example of love and righteousness, will truly bring about the fruit of freedom. Psalm 23 promises that our *Good Shepherd will, "guide us in the paths of righteousness for His name's sake."* He will never lead us astray.

MOVE IN THE OPPOSITE SPIRIT

Moving in the opposite spirit is a great warfare strategy in the Kingdom. Narcissism is based on selfishness, therefore death to self is the answer for victory. Narcissism is full of pride. Therefore, walking in humility is the greatest weapon against it. Narcissism is self-absorbed, therefore looking for ways to be attentive to the needs of others and sowing blessings into their lives in order to sincerely encourage them will defeat the spirit. If you take each and every symptom of narcissism and find the opposite behavior, **you *will* find the heart of God.**

When you intentionally move in the opposite spirit, you will make great headway in your war against narcissism.

RENEW THE MIND

The Word of God is powerful, and it both cleanses and renews the mind (Ephesians 4:22-24; 5:26-27). We are what we think, so it is important to align our thoughts with God's thoughts. God is void of all narcissistic beliefs. He is perfect and just in all His ways. As you read and proclaim the Word of God each day, your mind will be washed and renewed. Playing Bible CDs throughout your day and even while you sleep is also beneficial. Years ago I wrote a little book called Decree, a helpful tool for empowering believers. I continue to use that book to this very day.

The battlefield is in the mind and, therefore, Paul taught:

For though we walk in the flesh, we do not war according to the flesh, for the weapons of our warfare are not of the flesh, but divinely powerful for the destruction of fortresses. We are destroying speculations and every lofty thing raised up against the knowledge of God, and we are taking every thought captive to the obedience of Christ, and we are ready to punish all disobedience, whenever your obedience is complete. (2 Corinthians 10:3-6)

CAST OUT EVIL SPIRITS ASSOCIATED WITH NARCISSISM

Jesus declared that *signs would follow those who believe,* and one of those signs was the casting out of demons (see Mark 16:17). His commission to preach the Kingdom in Matthew 10:8 also included the casting out of demons. It is possible to cast them out of ourselves if we are believers in Christ. If you are not yet a born-again Christian, but you believe that Jesus is Lord and you desire Him to be your God and Savior, then simply invite Him to come into your heart, forgive your sins and give you new life. Feel free to pray the following prayer:

> ### Dear Lord Jesus,
> I believe that You are the Son of God
> and that You died on the cross for my sins.
> I want You alone to be my God and Savior.
> Please come into my heart and forgive all my sins.
> Make me a brand new creation in You
> and write my name in Your book of life.
> Thank You, Jesus, AMEN.

When you pray that prayer with sincere faith, Jesus will come into your life. He is now your God and Savior. You might feel His presence or you might not. Feeling is not the testing agent; your faith is. If you believe, then He is in you. He loves you! Your new life begins. He will transform you with His love and grace from the inside out.

With Christ now in your life, if you sense a controlling force in you that causes you to feel powerless to overcome, it is possible that an evil spirit might be controlling you. Do not be afraid. Simply cast it out like Jesus taught. Command every spirit of pride, selfishness, self-idolatry, self-absorption, narcissism and any others that you might discern, to come out in the name of Jesus. Command them to come out quietly. After you make the command in Jesus' name, believe that they have left. Sometimes it helps to expel them through the natural breath. Remember, "Greater is He who is in you than he who is in the world" (1 John 4:4). Wickedness is no match for righteousness. Jesus is the King of kings and no power can resist Him. (For more in-depth teaching and ministry on deliverance, order my *Catching the Thief* audio set and study guide.)

Don't be afraid to ask others to minister deliverance to you. Their love for you will release faith for your freedom, and oftentimes when you are bound, it is harder to see the areas within yourself.

BE FILLED WITH THE HOLY SPIRIT

Invite the Holy Spirit to fill you with His presence and power. He is so wonderful and will fill you with His divine nature. When you are filled and overflowing with the Holy Spirit, there is no room for the enemy or for bad thoughts and behavior patterns. Be filled continually. Throughout your day invite the Holy Spirit to come and fill you with power afresh. Whenever you feel weak, remember that He is strong. Receive His strength by faith.

QUESTIONS TO PONDER

1. Do you recognize narcissism in your own life – whether it's the actual disorder, a demonic bondage, or only several symptoms? Are you ready to overcome?

2. Write down who and how you have hurt others due to your narcissistic behavior. Write a prayer of personal repentance as well as a plan of action to reach out to those you are able to connect with. What steps do you need to take to rebuild relationship with those you continue to interact with?

3. Do you recognize the root of your narcissism as well as how it evolved? Based on the counsel given here, what is your plan of action to deal with it? Which of these can you do on your own and which will require you to seek help?

4. What was your main takeaway from this chapter and how will you respond to it?

CHAPTER FOUR

NARCISSISM IN
RELATIONSHIPS

I t is very challenging to engage in a relationship with someone who is narcissistic in their behavior. Relationships are to be founded on godly love, honor and respect for each other. The exchange is to be mutual. Individuals bound by narcissism most often relate with others mainly to benefit themselves. They cannot reciprocate love unless the results will bring them personal fulfillment or satisfaction.

As a result, people who are in a relationship with a narcissist will constantly suffer frustration, rejection, guilt, and shame. They often find themselves engaged in dysfunctional dynamics within the relationship. They are frequently motivated to please the narcissist in order to make them happy, keep the peace, or to gain their love and acceptance. I have known those in relationship with a narcissist to even lie on behalf of the narcissist in order to gain their approval.

Friendship with a narcissist is usually shallow, one-sided, unfulfilling and aggravating. Often individuals will be attracted to a narcissist due to their popularity and charismatic personality, but the relationship will always turn to that which supports the narcissist's needs for affirmation, attention, endorsement and association. If the personal benefit to the narcissist wanes in a friendship, the relationship usually is terminated or placed at arm's length by the narcissist.

A narcissist in the workplace or in a ministry position is normally extremely challenging and possibly even disastrous due to the self-absorbed and self-exalting motivation. They never labor with a pure motive to bless and encourage others unless it helps their agenda for success, increase, popularity or promotion. They can be competitive, prone to jealousy, and ostentatious, often creating strife in the workplace or ministry due to selfish agendas. Most of the time an individual struggling with narcissism is not teachable, and they resist discipline even if they seem to be in agreement outwardly. They beat to the sound of their own drum.

Being married to a person with narcissistic behavior is disappointing, unfulfilling, painful and often emotionally abusive. The spouse of a narcissist often lives with rejection, grueling demands and lack of attention. Some narcissists are very possessive and jealous of their spouses and therefore they control, emotionally manipulate and dominate them through shame and blame, while using them as showpieces to prop up their own image. A narcissist will always need more for themselves – more material things, more love, more attention, more praise, more time for themselves, more preferential treatment and more help. None of these will be enough, unfortunately. They seldom think of or care about the needs of their spouse unless it enhances their image or benefits them in some way.

The spouse of a narcissist can easily fall into dysfunction and often believes that if they just did a little bit more, performed a little bit better, were a little better looking or gave increased measures of affirmation and support, then perhaps their spouse would reciprocate their love, bringing peace and harmony into the marriage. A narcissist is unable to reciprocate with pure motives and they are never satisfied for long. As a result, the spouse faces constant disappointment, frustration, rejection, remorse and, at times, even abuse. Even though 75% of those diagnosed with NPD are male, females can also be affected. Both husbands and wives can be narcissistic.

The following list of behavior patterns are oftentimes found in a narcissistic spouse:

1. Acts out in verbally aggressive behaviors

2. When confronted or opposed, places blame or shame, accuses

3. Is insensitive to the needs of their spouse – the world revolves around them

4. Is controlling and manipulating

5. Shows rage or outbursts of anger when their spouse disagrees with them or makes them look bad in front of others

6. Often spends outside their budget, depends financially on their spouse, and asks for the spouse to help fund things for them. If the spouse withholds, they get upset and are often accusative and enraged. The opposite is also true for some. They are the breadwinners for the family but withhold finance from their spouse and use the household funds for their own goals, purposes, and pleasures.

7. Talks about themselves constantly and seldom seem interested in the life, needs or interests of their spouse

8. Expects special treatment from their spouse

9. Very sensitive if they are insulted even in the most subtle way (spouses usually feel like they are walking on thin ice and must be careful how they word things or voice complaints)

10. Shows one side of their personality in public but another side in private (they are hypocritical and can go out of their way to impress people)

11. Spouse can feel emotionally battered and confused

12. Spouses' self-esteem can diminish over time

Living with a Narcissist

While reading this book, you may recognize someone you know, perhaps even someone you live with, who manifests the symptoms of narcissism. Living with a narcissist can be extremely complex, as they desire to be loved and yet reject the one who loves them. They are incapable of truly loving others when bound by this spirit and mindset. It is difficult to live with the manipulations, deceptions, control, selfishness, and self-focus that are very much a part of the narcissistic person. The following are some points that might help encourage you. Remember that all things are possible when you believe in Jesus!

Do not blame yourself. A narcissist is unable to truly love. No matter how hard you try, it will never be enough. Their demands will never be satisfied. It is not your fault. Do not take responsibility for their shortcomings and behavior. Do **not** blame yourself.

Honesty and confrontation. Covering issues of narcissism and sweeping them under the carpet will not make them go away. Be honest with yourself about what you are facing. Sometimes shame or false guilt keeps us from being honest about the situation we are facing in our home, workplace or group. An honest assessment will give you a place to believe for solutions.

Relationships are built on honesty. Find a way to lovingly share your concerns. Many times a narcissist will kick back against confrontation, so don't shrink back should this happen. Sometimes you will need others to stand with you, as was described earlier, in an intervention type of setting.

Establish boundaries. A narcissist can make enormous demands on the emotions, time and gifts of those near to them. Do not be intimidated and pressured. Do not be afraid to say no. Establish your boundaries. Do not allow abusive assaults against your emotions, body, or sexuality in any way. If needed, share carefully with someone you trust, bringing the situation into the light in order to receive counsel and support.

There are times when individuals must give themselves some space and distance from the narcissist. A woman named Tina worked for a boss who was very narcissistic. She had addressed his negative and demeaning comments towards her a number of times, but he never apologized or even tried to change. In fact, when she addressed them, he would get angry and turn the blame back on her. These responses always confused her.

After many failed attempts to set boundaries, she had a heart-to-heart talk with him regarding the effect his words and behavior were having on her and others. He showed no remorse, and in fact he retaliated. He did not respect her boundaries or requests. Tina was confused and hurt but unwilling to live in such an atmosphere, so she resigned. She loved her job but did not want to allow the abuse, injustice and manipulation of her boss to affect her life at the workplace. She established her boundaries.

Love. Ultimately the power of true love will set the narcissist free if they are willing to receive it. True love, however, needs to be tough, confrontational and extremely honest at times. A strong commitment to love unconditionally will give you the grace to endure.

Forgiveness is an important part of love. I once ministered to a young woman whose husband had cheated on her. I shared with her about the power of forgiveness. She replied, "If I forgive him, I will be letting him off the hook." I responded and said, "No, my dear, you will be getting his hook out of you." Unforgiveness, bitterness, and offense will affect your health and well-being. We must forgive…and forgive…and forgive. You might not feel it, but you can choose it.

A young Christian woman I know lives in mid-America with a narcissistic husband. She became aware of his struggles through rude awakenings early in their marriage and since has believed God for his freedom. It has not been an easy journey. She established in her heart a strong, non-negotiable love covenant with her husband before God. Love always wants the best for the sake of another. Sometimes the best is not satisfying their every wish, or facilitating and/or covering inappropriate behavior. She learned to be loving, caring, kind, giving and gentle, yet confrontational when needed. She has maintained strong boundaries. From time to time, when her husband's responses were emotionally abusive, she would leave the home for a few days. One time she left for a few weeks in order to establish her boundaries and get re-empowered in love. On that occasion, she spent time praying for more grace, more love and more wisdom. She spoke to her husband over the phone and helped him reason through the situation while maintaining her clear position. She endeavored to help him see through a different lens. She never gave up and some change has come as a result.

Love never fails. Living with a narcissist will test your love and patience. If you pass the tests you will carry a strong authority and anointing in the essence, reality and power of love.

In the Walt Disney movie, "Beauty and the Beast," we see a prime example of narcissistic behavior.

The Beast was selfishly in love with himself at the exclusion of the welfare and happiness of others. Because of the curse that was put on him, he had to love someone (and be loved in return) or he would remain a beast forever. Being a narcissist, he could not love completely. *But with the pure and unselfish love of another* (Belle, who was unaware of her own beauty) *the Beast was set free to be the Prince again.* Not only would he now love (and be loved) completely, but his own appearance even transformed back to his original self.

Faith. All things are possible, only believe. Stand on the promises of God and believe for the Lord's intervention and deliverance with unwavering faith. Ultimately, each individual has a free will, but the Lord's grace is amazing. Never, never, never give up! A woman left her husband due to the abuse of narcissistic behavior, but she never stopped believing for his healing. To this day, there has been no evidence of change, but she is still standing in faith for her ex-husband's deliverance from narcissism. She has moved on with her life but is determined to never give up. She quietly and confidently stands in faith for his freedom.

Reward. Sometimes living with a narcissist can seem unbearable and constantly challenging. You must posture yourself to receive everything you need from the Lord. A narcissist is incapable of loving until they are set free. Therefore, you must receive your love directly from the Lord. A narcissist is unable to truly give encouragement unless it benefits them in some way, so you must receive your encouragement directly from the Lord. As you draw close to the Lord, you will be granted everything you need to live a good life. He IS your life! He is the One who will empower you, fulfill you and strengthen you. Isaiah 61:7 in *The Message* Bible says, "Because you got a double dose of trouble and more than your share of contempt, your inheritance in the land will be doubled and your joy goes on forever." Receive your reward by faith. In His presence you will find the fullness of joy.

Courage. Oftentimes people fear the narcissist due to their unpredictable rages, retaliations, and shame and blame techniques. God is not an accuser; He is a lover. Have the courage to face the reactions of the narcissist while maintaining your peace. You are loved and cherished and must fight to maintain that belief. If the situation is abusive, you will need the courage to walk away from the abuse and receive healing. You might need courage to disclose your situation to a friend or counselor. Darkness is empowered in secret. Be courageous and bring everything into the light.

Decree the Word. As mentioned earlier, the Word of God is powerful. In Isaiah 55:11, it states that the Word of God does not return empty but accomplishes its mission. When you make word decrees against narcissism, that word will go to work.

Job 22:28 says, "Decree a thing, and it will be established for you, and light will shine on your ways."

God's Word is a weapon — it is a sword and you can wield it well. Even as David slew Goliath with a stone and cut off his head with a sword, you can slay the giant of narcissism. You can. You will.

Have a support team. Dealing with a family member, friend, co-worker or acquaintance who is narcissistic can be draining. You need to be strong and firm and free from bitterness, offense, and resentment. Make sure that you get all the help and support you need. God does not want you to be a victim of narcissism but, rather, a victor over it.

In extreme cases you might need to seek out professional counsellors and therapists to give you insight into your situation.

Praise changes the atmosphere. I have found great breakthroughs in praise. Praise unto God lifts your soul but also releases breakthrough in the spirit. Paul and Silas experienced this in prison. They had been badly beaten and thrown into the inner, dark prison. They reacted by praising God. As they did, around midnight God intervened. Paul and Silas were set free, and ALL the prisoners were delivered from their captivity (Acts 16:25-26). Those bound by narcissism are in a spiritual prison. God can intervene through praise.

Pray in tongues. The gift of tongues is a supernatural gift of the Holy Spirit that enables you to speak in a heavenly language. You will not understand what you are saying when you pray in tongues, but the Spirit of God is releasing perfect prayer through your spiritual language. When one speaks in tongues, Scripture says that he "edifies himself" (1 Corinthians 14:4). When you live with a narcissist, you will need to be constantly built up in your faith. Praying in tongues will help you.

This gift is for every believer. If you do not speak in tongues, I highly recommend that you get the "Tongues" audio download or book (featured in the back of this book) as it will help you receive and utilize this wonderful gift. But you can simply ask the Holy Spirit right now, then step out in faith and speak in your new language.

Move on. You have a life to live. Your life is a gift to you and it doesn't have to be lived in the shadow of a narcissist. Live your life to the fullest in love, righteousness and honor. When you are filled with the Lord, knowing that all you need is found in Him, you are ready to move forward. There is a whole world out there for you to both impact and enjoy. You might feel called to remain in a situation with an undelivered narcissist in your life, but when you are secure in the Lord you will have everything you need to live in freedom in the midst of all the challenges you may face.

My husband and I had a prison ministry years ago. After we led prisoners to Jesus, they were still locked up in their cell at night, but because of their transformation, they were no longer confined by that cell. They enjoyed freedom as their new life unfolded. One night when we visited, an inmate was in tears after receiving Christ. He said, "I have spent years in prison, always longing for my freedom. I even attempted an escape. But since I received Christ, I have never known such great freedom. It is beyond anything I ever dreamt of. In or out of this building, I am free at last."

QUESTIONS TO PONDER

1. Do you have a day-to-day relationship with someone who is a narcissist or displays some of the symptoms? Who?

2. How has their behavior affected you and others? If this includes persons you are responsible for (your children, work subordinates, etc.), how have you helped them to deal with this situation? Are you satisfied with what you have been able to do, or do you recognize you need more support?

3. What have been your coping mechanisms? What boundaries have you placed?

4. Do you recognize the probable root(s) of this behavior (see previous chapter)? How has this affected your understanding of the person? Will it affect the way you deal with them in any way? Why and how?

5. In light of this (and/or previous) chapter(s), have you discovered some things you need to do that you hadn't done previously, or things you need to do differently? What is your plan of action to make these changes?

6. Do you have a church family and/or other people close to you who are knowledgeable of the situation and who encourage you and speak into your life?

7. What are two takeaways you have received from this chapter, and what will be your response?

CHAPTER FIVE

A FINAL WORD

In Christ, we are called more than conquerors. We are to be overcomers in this life. We are His light that expels darkness. We are the salt of the earth that preserves. The Word teaches us that nothing is too difficult for Him, and all things are possible to those who believe.

In the world we live in, there are many challenges. We don't need to look far to see them. We live in an immoral and corrupt society, *but there is always hope.* God is looking for a remnant of people who will stand strong, fight, and persevere in order to see righteousness and freedom abound. We are anointed like Jesus with the Holy Ghost and with power. Our call is to invade darkness with His light and set the captives free.

There are many who are held captive to narcissism. They are imprisoned by the deception of this wicked spirit and destructive, deceptive mindset. It is a demonic stronghold that we in Christ can and will break. Many in these days will receive total deliverance from the grip of this spirit. We will prevail. We will win!

Imagine the body of Christ full of believers who love each other perfectly, a body that always esteems one another other more than themselves, a body that is generous, kind, gentle and patient, and a people who are willing to lay down their lives for the well-being of another. Does this sound like Jesus? We are His body in the earth. This is what He is looking for.

A fire of purging is coming to the body of Christ (see Matthew 3:10-12; Isaiah 6:1-7; Malachi 3:2-3; 4:1). Everything that is not of love will be burned. Let's call for that purging fire now. Allow the dross to burn.

Lord Jesus,
Purge me of everything that is not of You, that is not of Your love. Send Your deliverance and Your purifying fire to every narcissistic thought, attitude, word, action and behavior pattern in my life, and in the lives of those I love. Cleanse me with the power of Your blood and forgiveness. Heal in me the things that hurt others, and make me a vessel of Your great love and power! AMEN.

1 CORINTHIANS 13

(The Message Bible)

Love never gives up.

Love cares more for others than for self.

Love doesn't want what it doesn't have.

Love doesn't strut,

Doesn't have a swelled head,

Doesn't force itself on others,

Isn't always "me first,"

Doesn't fly off the handle,

Doesn't keep score of the sins of others,

Doesn't revel when others grovel,

Takes pleasure in the flowering of truth,

Puts up with anything,

Trusts God always,

Always looks for the best,

Never looks back,

But keeps going to the end.

The Greatest Power... The Greatest Weapon...
The Greatest Person...
in the entire universe...
is LOVE.
Lord, reduce us to LOVE.

**Let's declare war on narcissism and believe for every
captive to be set free! Let the "love war" begin.**

BIBLIOGRAPHY

The Holy Bible (NASB and The Message)

The Narcissism Epidemic: Living in the Age of Entitlement (book) by-psychologists and professors Jean Twenge and W. Keith Campbell

Malignant Self Love – Narcissism Revisited (book) by Sam Vaknin

Online Encyclopedia Britannica

Wikipedia, the free dictionary

Genealogical Guide to Greek Mythology by Carlos Parada

Meaning from Madness: Understanding the Hidden Patterns that Motivate Abusers: Narcissists, Borderlines, and Sociopaths (book) by Richard Skerritt

Resource items that will help you grow (more information in the back pages of this book):

Decree book

Decree audio

The Spiritual Cleanse audio download

Catching the Thief audio set and study guide

Tongues audio and book

BONUS BOOK:

God Loves You
With an Everlasting Love

1

THE GOD KIND OF LOVE

Behold what *manner* of love the Father has bestowed on us, *that we should be called children of God* (1 John 3:1a NKJV, emphasis added).

What manner of love would motivate a perfect, holy, and righteous God to offer a sinful, rebellious person the right to become His very own dear child and heir of all that He is and all that He has? It sounds like an extravagant act, doesn't it? This, however, is indeed the very manner of love the Father has shown to each and every one of us. Nothing throughout all the history of mankind has ever been able to make Him withdraw this love, although we have all put His love to the test over and over again. The demonstration of this love is unchangeable because He is unchangeable.

Many individuals regularly waver in their assurance of God's love and continually question their right standing with Him. The lack of this assurance breeds insecurity. They might ask, "Am I worthy enough? Do I love God enough? Am I performing well enough? Am I serving Him enough?"

My faith constantly wavered just like this before I understood the clear revelation of Christ's work on the Cross that demonstrated His eternal, unchangeable love for me. During those years, I always questioned my value in His sight. This produced striving, tension, and unrest. Without the assurance of His unchanging love, you are never free to be. If you are not free to be, you will never be free to do. It is the revelation of His love that produces fullness, freedom, and fruitfulness in life.

First John 4:16-19 teaches us that "There is no fear in love... We love Him because He first loved us." When you understand the unconditional love of God, the fear of not being accepted and loved by Him is eliminated. You know deep within that you're His precious one, and you're assured of your place in His heart forever. When you have this type of assurance, even when everything in your life is unsettled, you feel secure. Love gives you an unshakeable confidence that He will work everything out and keep you in perfect peace.

Romans 8:32-39 informs us that the love the Father has given us is greater than any other force. It confidently assures us that nothing can separate us from His love. In fact, you can never be separated from the love of God that is in Christ Jesus – NEVER. In Christ, you are forever sealed in His holy love. Oh, how wonderful!

You perhaps weren't loved unconditionally in your childhood (just as many others weren't), so from time to time these lying thoughts might have assaulted your mind: I'm not loveable. I'm not accepted. I haven't been able to accomplish enough. I have no value. I can't succeed.

The Word, however, says that you are perfectly loved, and nothing at all can ever separate you from it. When you really start to understand this truth, you will be able to cast down the tormenting lies of rejection, inferiority, and insecurity. The power of God's love and favor will prevail, causing the lies to fall. Then you will experience what you were created to be from the foundation of the world – an object of His deep love and affection.

God wants you to feel so secure in His love that you will be able to go anywhere, do anything, face any spirit of rejection, and overcome any obstacle. You will be able to say with confidence, "I am a precious, loved child of God. I am His favored one."

Love is God's mark on our lives. Not only are we to know His love for ourselves, but we are to extravagantly share it with others. Once you know you are a loved one, His love in you will spill out all over the place and touch others – you won't be able to help it! This type of love doesn't come from an inward striving to be a loving person. It comes from knowing who you are as a perfectly loved child. Then His powerful grace flows through you like a river and offers refreshing to those around you.

A PERSONAL TESTIMONY

I remember so clearly what life was like without Christ and the revelation of His love. I was a young career woman, a wife and a mother of two boys, yet totally unfulfilled and broken. Most of my brokenness, however, was hidden to the onlooker. I wore an invisible mask of well-being because I was afraid to let people see the real me. What if they rejected me? How could I ever cope with that? I constantly lived behind the many disguises that concealed the guilt and shame plaguing my heart regularly. I was in an invisible prison and I couldn't escape.

I tried everything to become free. I attended numerous self-help courses and joined new age/occult enlightenment groups, hoping to find some answers for my distressed soul. I regularly imbibed a variety of addictive substances in an effort to find comfort and relief.

I also attempted to find meaning for life through work, career, and taking extra college courses. Every effort failed terribly to offer any liberty. I became increasingly unstable emotionally, with no way to get a grip on things. The more I tried, the more I failed. The more I failed, the more discouraged and bound I became. The tentacles of fear, shame, and guilt wrapped themselves around me, continuously strangling any tinge of hope. I was constantly plagued with a sense of powerlessness in life.

I was a mess and totally out of control! I desperately needed help but didn't know where to turn. God hears the cries of our heart, and He definitely heard mine. It was following a near-death experience, at the lowest point of my life, that the Lord sent a wonderful man to share the gospel with me. He was an Anglican minister named Reverend Ron Hunt. I will never forget the first evening I attended the little home Bible study at his invitation. Although I was nervous to step into that unfamiliar environment, I was pleasantly surprised as I witnessed a sincere group of people who obviously knew God in a very personal way. One after another that evening, they shared testimonies of how Jesus had changed their lives. They claimed that He forgave their sins, cleansed them from guilt and shame, and offered them a brand new life. Wow! That was exactly what I wanted ... but was it possible?

Following the meeting, I went home and while alone kneeling on my living room floor, I cried out to this unseen God for help. "Jesus, I have nothing to offer You except my brokenness. I have made a big mess of my life, but I would really like You to come into my heart and make me new – just like You did for those people up the street." I honestly did not know if Jesus would want to come into my life or not. I felt so evil and had no confidence that He would be able to love the likes of me. Yet, to my amazement, He didn't hesitate to enter my heart. I hadn't even finished praying when I literally felt the presence of liquid love come into my being. The One who knew every wicked detail of my life didn't hesitate for a moment to show me His extravagant mercy and acceptance. I felt the pressure of my sin leave me, along with all the guilt and shame. It was as though a prison door had been opened and I was allowed to run free. I felt lovely and beautiful inside for the very first time I could remember.

All I could do was cry. In fact, I cried all night while I worshipped Him. No one had to teach me to worship – when you are deeply touched by His love, worship is just a normal response... it is the only response! Everything in you is so thankful, so grateful. I knew beyond a shadow of a doubt that this gift of love had nothing to do with my own ability to fix myself. I had already proven through constant failed attempts that I was "unfixable." This gift had nothing to do with me. This was a free gift of life – His gift of everlasting, unbendable, unchangeable, unshakable, and unfailing love! Yeah, God!

The next number of years were extremely fulfilling for me as I daily experienced increased revelation of His Word and His ways. His love healed, delivered, and established me in a brand new life. It had nothing at all to do with my efforts. This new life was His gift. It is a gift that can't be earned and it is available to everyone. It is available to you!

I began to serve the Lord with passion. I never for a moment felt a pressure to serve Him – I served Him because I loved Him. It's what you do when you're in love. My entire life changed. I had new friends, new interests, and new desires. I wanted to spend my entire life serving the One who had loved me so perfectly. Year after year was filled with a continual unfolding of His goodness.

In my experience as a young Christian, I had never tasted "legalism" (legalism is an attempt to secure right standing with the Lord through obedience to the Law). I was first introduced to this type of religious bondage when our family served the Lord on a foreign mission field (my husband had begun following Jesus a year after me). The leaders of the mission center were very passionate for the Lord, and I know they meant well. Unfortunately, they did not understand that the Lord's unconditional love is a gift and cannot be earned through our works. As a result, they taught those they worked with to perfect themselves through self-effort in order to please God. The leaders themselves also lived under this same burden. I experienced a daily performance pressure on this mission field.

In all my striving to do well, I constantly believed I was falling short of what was expected. I was convinced I was disappointing God, and the more I tried to please Him the more I failed. The more I failed, the more I strove within. The cycle continued with increasing despair. This type of pressure was bringing me right back into the torment and bondage I experienced prior to knowing Christ. I was plagued with the same guilt and the same shame. It simply showed up wearing different clothes. One was a cloak of unrighteousness, and the other was one of self-righteousness. Both were deadly and bore the same fruit of devastation.

After serving on this mission field as faithfully and diligently as I could for over six months, I finished our term feeling spiritually bankrupt. I had even lost assurance of my salvation. I believed I had totally failed the Lord and that He would never have any use for me again. I believed that I was no longer a precious child to Him – I had disappointed Him too deeply. What a deception I had stepped into!

On my return home from this mission experience, some friends helped me to rightly divide the Word and to trust that the Lord still loved me. The healing and restoration did not come overnight. At times I was still plagued with the fear of being rejected by God, and I constantly battled self-condemnation. I cried out constantly for relief. All I wanted was to feel close to God – to feel worthy of His love and to know I was pleasing Him.

It was years later that I finally received a revelation of the Cross. This revelation delivered me from the torment and fear that had bound my soul. The new revelation became an anchor for my faith forever. The revelation of the Cross and the covenant Christ made with God on our behalf is an absolute foundation for understanding His unconditional love. The day I received this revelation, I wept for hours on end, completely in awe of His loving kindness – completely amazed at His grace.

It is one thing to be touched by the love of God and enjoy the experience of it, like I had as a young Christian. It is another thing, however, to be fully anchored in the unshakable, unfailing revelation of the doctrine of His unconditional love. Jesus said, "You will know the truth, and the truth will make you free" (John 8:32). The day the revelation of the doctrine of the Cross filled my heart was the day I knew I would walk free forever. Regardless of what circumstances surrounded my life, regardless of how many condemning thoughts my mind received, I now had an eternal place to stand. I was anchored forever in His love because I understood the truth of it! I am blood-bought into an eternal love covenant that can never be broken. What freedom this truth brings!

In this writing, I am committed to introducing you to this life-changing, life-sustaining doctrine. May you come to know the revelation of this truth so deeply within your heart that your entire being will forever be filled and anchored in it. I desire you to walk through the following pages with expectation and focus as the Holy Spirit unfolds the most profound and life-altering doctrine in the entire Bible – the Cross and the Covenant. This doctrine reveals God's true heart of unfailing, tested love. He loves you with an everlasting love. He really does. You will see!

2

GOD CHOSE YOU!

God wanted you! You weren't a mistake, regardless of the circumstances that surrounded your birth. Perhaps you weren't planned by your parents, or maybe your conception was the result of an unfortunate incident. Even in cases as sad as these, you need to know that God had you in His heart from before the foundation of the world. He planned you. His ultimate desire was for you to be conceived and brought forth in a beautiful, pure atmosphere of parental love and affection. Tragically, everyone has fallen short of His perfect ways because of our sinful, imperfect nature. God planned for you to come forth into the realm of time and fulfill His eternal purpose for your life. His potential in you is fun to explore.

God actually wanted to have a family. That's why most folks desire to have children; that desire comes from Him. Mankind has been created in His likeness and, therefore, when you find yourself longing to have children, you are simply identifying with His passion. He wanted children, and that's why you do, too (unless you've been emotionally wounded or have a special call to remain single).

In the beginning, God created trees, flowers, birds, fish, animals, and a host of other earthly and celestial things. He loved everything He created and each day He said, "It is good." Even though He was

93

very pleased, He still longed for a precious creation made in His likeness – an object of His affection to fulfill the longing of His righteous heart. My husband Ron and I did not have children in our first year of marriage. We did, however, have pets – two dogs.

Although we enjoyed our dogs and they were like family, they did not satisfy our longing for children. The dogs were nice, but not that nice. There was something inside us that said, "Children, children, children." That longing was a small taste of what the Lord felt in His heart for us. The dogs and other creatures were not enough for Him, either. Although He took pleasure in them, they did not satisfy His desire to have YOU! Passionate desire for you was burning inside His heart. Envisioning you, He said, "I long for you; I desire to pour out My deep love, kindness, and goodness upon you."

God deeply desired children, yet before man was ever created, God knew we were going to blow it. He wasn't caught off guard, though – He is the all-knowing One. As a result of knowing ahead of time about our sinful failures, before He even created us He initiated a plan to rescue our lives from the power of sin. This act is called "redemption" in the Bible. He actually took care of the problem for us before we had even acted out the problem (the Lamb was slain before the foundation of the world – Revelation 13:8). God has never been caught off guard by mankind's failures – and that includes yours!

Years ago, I said to the Lord, "I wouldn't choose to have children if I knew ahead of time they were going to rebel, betray, and dishonor me. I would be much happier without that type of child! Why then did You create us?" He spoke this clear word to me:

94

My plan was to prove to mankind that My love would withstand every resistance. I allowed My love to be tested so that you would know it would always stand and never be withdrawn. I am Love.

When anyone chooses to come into relationship with Me, they will never ever need to doubt My love for them. Knowing I passed every test, they will feel completely secure – and that is My desire.

That's how much He loves you. Isn't that amazing? Behold, what manner of love is this?

THE CROSS AND THE COVENANT

God's plan for you is to have an eternal relationship with Him that is established through a covenant. A covenant is a legally binding agreement between two people or parties. In order for a covenant to work, there needs to be absolute integrity in the making and keeping of all its terms. Entering a covenant with a person of integrity gives you a sense of protection, a sense of security.

That's what the marriage covenant is supposed to be like. When you vow to be faithful to one another, to care for one another, and honor each other, you should feel a sense of belonging and oneness with your covenant partner. That is the purpose of covenant. It legally secures relationship.

Mankind does not have a history of being good covenant keepers, so the very thing that should offer security is making many feel insecure. Some don't even bother getting married anymore because they think it might last or it might not. That is one reason why there is so much breakdown in the family these days. There are broken covenants everywhere, and this is evidenced by the high divorce rate in our nation. God, however, is a covenant-keeping God. He is full of integrity and always keeps the terms of the covenants He makes.

The original use of the word covenant was, "where the blood flows." Ancient covenants always set terms, exchanged names, weapons, and resources. These covenants almost always included the consummation of the covenant through the mingling of blood. A covenant meal was served at the end of the ceremony and a celebration of this union commenced.

The marriage covenant is a blood covenant much like this. We make our vows before witnesses (which is an exchanging of terms), we exchange names (the bride usually takes her husband's name), and we exchange our resources (the assets of one legally become the other's, in most cases). The marriage is then consummated through the sexual act, which breaks the hymen membrane (the shedding of blood). God's covenant plan for His relationship with man was a blood covenant (Christ's blood shed for us at the Cross). He set the terms, (through the Old Testament Law and Prophets) and then defined a name exchange (Jesus said, "In my name, ask ..."), a weapons exchange (Jesus' weapons and armor are ours), and a resource exchange (all our needs are met through Him).

In ancient civilizations, a representative of one tribe would cut covenant with a representative of another tribe. When the two leaders cut covenant on behalf of their people, then their entire tribe enjoyed the benefits of the covenant. This is what Christ did for us when He represented mankind in a covenant with God. Jesus Christ was and is our covenant representative and leader. It is His responsibility, as our covenant representative, to keep all the terms for us. In exchange, we receive all the covenant blessings. Wow!

3

THE AMAZING GOOD NEWS

What I'm about to share with you is amazing. God desired to make a covenant with man that would secure us in relationship with Him for all eternity. However, He knew that once mankind fell, we would never keep a covenant. It was impossible, because man became filled with a sin nature. To fulfill the covenant terms, God required a sinless representative for man who would keep all the conditions, but there was not a sinless person to be found. As a result, He chose to fill this position Himself. He chose to take our place in covenant by becoming a man. Jesus also took God's place in covenant because He is God. He is both man and God. In reality then, He was cutting covenant with Himself. This is how God could cut an eternal, unbreakable, unfailing covenant with man. Jesus, who was fully God, left heaven and came into the sinful world as a man in order to fulfill this plan.

Many Christians don't understand this, so I pray the light will go on for you today, because this truth is glorious. When you understand, you will worship and serve Him in full abandonment for all He has done. God loves you so much. He desires relationship with you even more than you desire relationship with Him. He knew you couldn't keep a covenant, so He determined to become man and fulfill both sides of the covenant Himself. Jesus, the Son of God and

Son of Man, made a covenant to include you in eternal relationship because you couldn't do it yourself.

When He came as a man, He had to fulfill all of man's covenant terms which were laid out in Old Testament Law. If He failed to fulfill every point of the Law, or if He gave in to temptation just once, He would not qualify to keep the covenant on man's behalf. This would have been devastating for us, but there was an even greater risk for Him. Jesus is referred to in Scripture as the last Adam. The first Adam was a perfect man before the fall. He was made in God's image and likeness. When he fell into temptation, the rule and dominion that had been given to him was surrendered over to Satan. Romans 6:16 teaches that when we submit ourselves to sin, we become sin's slave. This is what happened to Adam when he submitted to Satan's temptation, and this is what would have happened to the last Adam (Jesus), too, if He fell into even the slightest temptation. Only pure love would be willing to take a risk like that.

JESUS THE MAN

Jesus came just like the first Adam. He was of man's nature yet without sin. He was to fulfill man's requirement in covenant – with man's power and with man's capabilities. The Holy Spirit came upon Him to empower Him, just like the Holy Spirit empowers you today. Through the power of the Holy Spirit, the man, Jesus, remained sinless throughout His entire life on the earth. You need to understand that He resisted sin in man's strength, with the power of the Holy Spirit helping Him. You'd better believe that there was a huge wrestle in His soul against sin, even though He was perfect and without sin in His nature. He had to wrestle just like the first Adam, because

He had to secure the victory as a man in order to restore mankind to his rightful place in relationship with God. Ultimately, Jesus Christ, at the end of His "covenant course," would be acknowledged not only as a perfect God but also as a perfect Man who would sit on a throne at the right hand of God. All things in heaven and in earth would ultimately be summed up in Him.

It was not easy for Christ to resist sin. In fact, at one point it was so grueling that He sweat drops of blood in His resistance against the temptations (Hebrews 12:4). He did it in man's power for you so you wouldn't have to do it, because you couldn't do it. Everything required for mankind to enter covenant with God was fulfilled through the man Jesus Christ. Jesus fulfilled all the Law and the Prophets.

JESUS COUNTS THE COST

Before the foundation of the world, Jesus probably had to ask Himself, "How big is My love? Am I willing to perform acts of love, kindness, and mercy for people who don't even desire Me? Am I able to love so deeply that I would actually become sin for those whom I love? Am I willing to taste death for them?" He counted the cost and made a love choice with you in mind, saying, "Oh, yes! You are worth everything to Me. I will gladly leave heaven and pay the price, with joy!"

JESUS ARRIVES ON EARTH

Mary, a young virgin, conceived Jesus by the power of the Holy Spirit. She and Joseph traveled to Bethlehem, where Mary went into labor. There was no available lodging, so Mary gave birth in an animal stable and laid baby Jesus in a feeding trough. What kind of treatment was this for man's Savior? No palace, no special treatment, and hardly anyone even discerned who He was.

He had to start passing love tests right away. If He had been offendable, He could have thought: *Well, that's it, I'm going back to heaven. I tried to do something nice for you, but you treated Me like an animal and threw Me in a feeding trough.* Jesus, however, did not take offense. In tremendous humility, He passed the love test. Even though He was worthy of the most extravagant treatment, He didn't demand it or expect it. He came to serve.

Herod even tried to have Him killed as a baby, but Jesus never stopped loving. He never withdrew love and never lost faith. What would you do if your only motivation was to help people and all of a sudden they're trying to kill you? You'd probably say something like, "I don't need you. I'll go somewhere else." But Jesus had a different heart.

His Ministry Begins

His childhood passed and His ministry began. He taught in the synagogues as a rabbi. The religious leaders examined His teachings carefully. They knew the Scriptures and were considered experts in the Word of God and doctrine. Jesus, however, is true doctrine. He is the living Word. He is true theology and yet He was called a blasphemer and a heretic by these very leaders. They attempted to bring legal charges against Him. This is the way they treated the true God.

How would you feel if you were God? There you are, teaching truth right from heaven. You're speaking truth because you *are* truth, and the people you came to save are saying, "You're a liar. You're a deceiver. You're a heretic. You're teaching us false doctrine.

You're demonized." Character assaults like this are much worse than simply saying, "Your theology is off."

I've experienced a little of that resistance myself and I must say those times were brutal. Everything in me wanted to withdraw. Jesus, however, never withdrew love from us, not for a moment. Each time He was opposed or mistreated by man, His love once again passed the test. He said, "I will never withdraw love and I will never stop believing in what can happen in your life." He kept consistent in faith and love through all the mistreatment.

Jesus chose twelve disciples and then seventy-two. He poured His time and life into them by giving, teaching, and mentoring day in and day out. Many others also followed His ministry. His own didn't always treat Him well, but even with all the disappointments He suffered, He never wavered in His commitment to them.

4

Love's Greatest Tests

The Garden of Gethsemane

One of Christ's most excruciating struggles was in Gethsemane (Gethsemane means "the oil press"). He faced every temptation that man would ever encounter. Strong forces of hell were spiritually assaulting Him. As we established earlier, Jesus had to resist sin as a man – in the same strength as the first Adam. You were in His heart the entire time He was wrestling against temptation. The pressure was so great against His soul that He sweat blood in His resistance against sin. With every drop of blood that pushed through His bursting capillaries, He was saying, "For you, I will resist. No matter what it feels like. No matter how excruciating it is. My emotions are being wrung out beyond explanation, but it's all for you. It's all for you."

I've faced some grueling spiritual battles and have engaged in warfare with powerful demonic entities. Although these seasons were unbearably painful, they were nothing at all in comparison to what Jesus experienced. I am a little aware, however, of the crushing feeling that pressures your emotions and your mind during such times. In the midst of this type of battle, it is essential to keep focused, because all you have is the Word of God to stand on. When everything else that is going on in your life seems contrary to the truth, there's just one point of choice: "I will stand on Your Word, Lord, no matter what. I will trust my soul into Your keeping." It is all you have. At the end of these battles, your emotions, your thinking processes, and even your physical body is weakened, fatigued, and fragile. At times during these intense battles, I had to draw strength from God to even breathe. The impact of such warfare is very excruciating; I can't even find words to describe it. What I experienced, however, is still nothing in comparison to the pressure that Jesus experienced.

What was it like for Jesus when He had the hordes of hell trying to take Him out? What motivated Him to stand through this agony? God didn't *need* to put Himself in this position. Do you know why He did? It was His love for you. He said, "I'm doing this to fulfill your covenant requirements." He loves you that much. Just for a moment, forget about everyone else on the face of the earth. If you alone were left, He'd do it all over again. In the midst of Gethsemane's agony, you were in His vision. The thought of having you with Him for all eternity was His motivation to continue. Your face gave Him the strength to endure.

BETRAYED BY A FRIEND

When Jesus departed from the garden, He was weak and exhausted. Judas, one of His twelve disciples, approached Him, betraying Him with a kiss. Even though Jesus knew Judas would betray Him, He continued to call him friend. He said, "Friend, do what you have come for." (Matthew 26:50) Betrayal is very painful. If you have been betrayed, you know how difficult this is on your emotions, but even betrayal could not make Jesus withdraw love or friendship. There is nothing you can do to make Him withdraw His love. You can treat God terribly. You can tell Him to leave you alone, but He will never withdraw love from you. He'll continue to say, "I love you."

ABANDONED AND DENIED

I can't imagine what it would feel like to be in a ferocious spiritual battle and then experience betrayal by a close friend and co-worker. To top it all off, though, all His followers fled when He was arrested. When you're in a hard place, being falsely accused, you just want someone, even if it's only one, to stand with you. *Is there one that will just come to My side right now? Is there one who will believe in Me? Is there one who will defend Me?* Jesus did not even have one. His own disciples, whom He had poured into for three years, all fled in fear for their reputation.

As Jesus was led away, He heard Peter, one of His closest disciples, swearing, "No, I never knew Him." Oh how painful it must have been for Jesus when He heard that denial. He knew prophetically that Peter would do this, but foreknowledge doesn't ease the emotional devastation when it actually happens.

> *Peter, I need you right now. Are you so afraid for your own life that you wouldn't even admit you know Me? Peter, look into My eyes and see My pain. See My love. You have denied Me, but You cannot make Me withdraw love from you.*

His Trial

False witnesses were paid to testify against Jesus in court. That is harsh! When you know someone is lying about you, the natural tendency is to immediately defend yourself. Isaiah 53:7 reveals, though, that Jesus was like a lamb led to the slaughter, silent before His shearers, not opening His mouth in His own defense. He had purposed in His heart to offer unconditional love and mercy toward the lying witnesses.

You can line your pockets with filthy lucre, but you cannot make Me withdraw My love from you.

They stripped Him naked, placed a crown of thorns on His head and mocked Him openly. Even though you and I were not yet created, we were there, hidden in the heart of depraved humanity. We might think that we would never hurt or deny Him but, like Peter, we might not understand the weakness of our own flesh. It is probable that each of us would have done the same thing.

Christ's love was being severely tested by mankind. You and I have put His love to the test many times, and yet He has never abandoned us and neither has He withdrawn His love. He never will.

Beaten and Scourged

Jesus was beaten, spit upon, and mocked. His face was violently struck, apparently making Him unrecognizable. Again, with every cruel punch, His response was only love as He gazed into the eyes of His afflicters.

He was brutally scourged with a whip that had nine leather strips. At the end of each strip were little pieces of sharp metal or bone. Each stroke provided nine lashings. It was a common belief that 40 lashes would bring death. Under Roman laws, He might have received even more. History reveals that His flesh was literally ripped open and that His innards were exposed. Every time the razor-sharp edge of the whip dug into His flesh, you were in His heart. Your face was constantly before Him. You were the reason He could endure such hostility. Looking into the face of those who were cruelly scourging Him, He would have said once again, "You cannot make Me withdraw My love." He would have assured you, too, if it was your hand holding the scourge.

CRUCIFIED

Jesus carried the heavy wooden cross that was heaved onto His back. Weakened with pain, He staggered up to Calvary's Hill. An angry mob followed Him, mocking, ridiculing and shouting, "Crucify Him, crucify Him." They nailed His hands and feet to the cross and hung Him between two guilty criminals. They were crucifying an innocent man.

To many, it looked like Jesus' life was being taken. It appeared that Jesus was defeated, but His life wasn't taken – *it was given!* The devil did not take Jesus' life. The false witnesses did not take His life. The Jews did not kill Him. The Romans did not kill Him. You did not kill Him. No one killed Him. He freely gave His life. When you see Jesus hanging on the cross, you see Love Himself hanging there – a free gift of love – love that had been completely proven and tested against everything that could possibly oppose or destroy it.

Love Himself was on that cross, stripped naked and humiliated, hanging there in agonizing pain. In the midst of this agony, one of the thieves asked to be saved. Jesus didn't hesitate. In His greatest point of need, He continued to pour Himself out. He could have said, "What do you mean, you want a favor from Me? Really? I don't deserve to be here, and you do. Forget it, it's too late!" Jesus wasn't and isn't like that. He proved His love once again: "Of course, I will save you. In fact, today I'll do it and you will be with Me in paradise. You will see the glory of My salvation."

Looking down from His cross, Jesus saw a mass of people – a crowd who delighted to watch Him die. "If You're the Son of God, come down off that cross and save Yourself." His merciful, loving retaliation was, 'Father, forgive them; for they do not know what they do." (Luke 23:34)

Can you imagine? We sometimes find it difficult to forgive those who hurt or offend us. Consider Jesus: a mass of angry people rallied against Him, and you were there, too – all humanity was. Oh yes, He saw your face in the crowd that day. We all sinned against Him, and yet He said, "Father, forgive them all." He forgave all the sins of mankind right at that point. He cancelled the debt of sin. Only pure Love Himself can do that.

He went even further and actually became mankind's sin. Jesus chose to become sin. He chose to have your sin poured into Him so that He could pour His righteousness into you. He chose to become something abhorrent that would be judged, so you would be free from judgment. Have you ever been mistreated, taken advantage of, or sinned against? Doesn't it give you a great feeling to see the offender punished, knowing they're getting what they deserve? But Jesus' heart was different. He said, "No, I'll take the punishment for your sin. I'll take full responsibility. You can go free."

A number of years ago, I was on the mission field. I misjudged a particular situation and consequently made some bad decisions. My actions seriously hurt some individuals. When I finally saw the situation clearly, I was terribly grieved, overwhelmed, and deeply ashamed. I thought: I should have known better, I shouldn't have done that. It was difficult for me to believe that I hadn't seen the situation through eyes of wisdom in the first place. I asked for forgiveness from one individual who was particularly wounded through the process. They refused to extend the undeserved mercy that I desperately needed. For years afterward, I had a very difficult time forgiving myself.

One day, I was crying out to the Lord in prayer, "Don't let my failure continue to hurt them. Don't let it ruin their lives." I felt terrible to the very core of my being.

The Lord spoke very soberly to me, "You didn't commit that sin. You didn't make that mistake. I did."

"What? No, Lord! You never did that. I'm the one who did it."

"I did it," He insisted.

"Jesus, no You didn't. You are perfect and You have never wronged anyone, ever!"

He tenderly responded, "I bore your mistake on the Cross 2,000 years ago. I chose to take full responsibility for this mistake so that you might go free. I have even borne the judgment for it. You are free! I became this sin for you and, in exchange, I have given you My righteousness. This has all been paid in full. If there is any further problem, that hurting individual will need to come to Me. You have been totally released and fully justified. You never did it!"

I burst into tears, tears of gratitude that flowed from deep inside my being. How can I not love a God who showed that much mercy? He clearly revealed to me that day that this is what He's done for us all. This is what is called "substitution." He literally took our judgment and in exchange, gave us His life and righteousness. Oh my, can we fully grasp this?

5

FOR ALL PEOPLE AND
FOR ALL TIME

God's love for us today is no different than it was for the sinful crowd at the foot of the cross 2,000 years ago. He performed an eternal exchange, saying, "It is no longer you that sinned, but Me. I have become your sin. I have paid the penalty. I have taken full responsibility. It is no longer your issue." Love laid down His life for all people. Love laid down His life for you! You are free!

DYING IN FAITH

Gazing at you through the portals of time, Jesus died on the cross in love and in faith. He gave up the ghost and cried out, "It is finished." Helpless, but remaining in faith, He entrusted His life into the hands of His Father. When He became your sin, He had no power to raise Himself from the dead. God planned Christ's resurrection before the foundation of the world. And Jesus believed Him.

After His death, Jesus descended into the lower parts of the earth. On the third day, His heavenly Father raised Him from the dead. Mary and the other women, the disciples, and many others, literally saw Him walking the earth following His resurrection. Oh yes, He is the Resurrection and the Life – the First Born from the dead! When He was raised from the dead, He took the keys of death and of hell. He stripped the devil of his authority and made an open show of him. Oh, what an eternal victory!

Jesus Christ Is Forever the Resurrection and the Life

Jesus has invited everyone into eternal relationship with God through simply receiving Him as Savior by faith. All the work for mankind's redemption has been completed in Christ – finished! He did it all for us. The only thing left for us to do is to simply believe. Mankind's identity is found in Jesus – the One who accomplished everything for us. No man can boast in his own ability to save himself. Jesus fully paid the debt that we could not pay. He fully accomplished the work that we could not do. All glory to Him!

Jesus walked the earth for 40 days after His resurrection from the dead and then gloriously ascended to heaven. He is forever seated at the right hand of God, far above all principalities, powers, and every name that is named (Ephesians 1:20-22). We are seated with Jesus in the heavenly places when we receive Him as our Savior (Ephesians 2:6). Our life is hidden with Christ in God (Colossians 3:3).

Sealed in the Covenant

Everyone who believes in Christ has the gift of everlasting life – His abundant life. Everyone who believes in Him is forever sealed into covenant, a legally binding love agreement between God and man. This covenant is an eternal covenant. It is impossible for it to be broken because it is between Jesus, Man and Jesus, God. Jesus won our place for us through His own sinless life. When you believe in Him, you are saved from the separation from God that sin creates. Your identity as a Kingdom child is not in your own ability to accomplish anything. It is in His completed work – His ability – past tense. It is done! It is finished!

In fact, if we were to be absolutely honest right now, you are an utter failure outside of Christ. It is impossible for you to please God in your own strength – absolutely impossible! The only way anyone can please God is by believing in Christ. The arms of Jesus are open to all sinners. If you receive Jesus as Savior, then your identity is in Him. You are in Christ, a brand new creation. You are eternally one with Him. It is simple faith that connects you to this glorious eternal salvation. That's all you have to do – simply believe. That's it. That's all. Ephesians 2:8-9 says, "For by grace you have been saved through faith, and that not of yourselves; it is the gift of God, not of works, lest anyone should boast."

What is this grace that saves us? It is His divine influence in your life. It is His choice to accomplish everything for you. It is His work of favor over you – undeserved favor. You don't deserve it, I don't deserve it. No one does. It's undeserved, unmerited favor. It's His influence that comes upon your heart. You have been saved by grace through faith. Simple faith is what connects you to the glorious, finished work of the Cross. When you make this "faith connection," you become a brand new creation. Second Corinthians 5:17 states, "Therefore, if anyone *is* in Christ, *he is* a new creation; old things have passed away; behold, all things have become new."

Ah, what a glorious life we have been given in Christ – a brand new life, an eternal relationship with God Himself. Christ did all this for YOU! You see how precious you are? God loves you with an everlasting love ... He really does!

Perhaps you have just read this through, and your heart is longing to become God's child. It's simple. The following is a little prayer. If it represents your desire, why don't you go ahead and pray it from your heart. God will hear you. His gift of life and love will enter you, and your journey begins!

DEAR HEAVENLY FATHER,

Thank You for loving me so perfectly through Your Son, Jesus Christ, and for offering me eternal life through the finished work of the Cross. I turn away from a self-ruled life and invite Jesus Christ to enter my heart as my personal Savior and Lord.

Come into my life, Lord Jesus, and forgive me of all my sin. Give me new life within and make me the person You want me to be. I believe that You are now in my heart and my new life has begun. I now belong to You. You are my God. Thank You, Father. AMEN.

YOUR NEW LIFE BEGINS

When you receive Jesus as your personal Savior by faith, His life enters your spirit. You are now what the Scripture calls *born again* (Read John 3:1-9). You have Christ's brand new life inside you. His purity, love, peace, truth, and blessings are now inside your spirit. You are so beautiful and perfect within.

Just like a new baby in the natural needs nourishment and care, so do new babies in the Lord. The Bible is full of truth that is like fresh milk and food for you. As you read it each day, it will nourish you and reveal wonderful things about God's love and His ways. You will also want to meet some other Christians who understand the love of God. Fellowshipping with other followers of Jesus is so much fun. Take some time and visit some churches in your area. Christ's Holy Spirit dwells within you, and He will direct you to a good fellowship if you ask Him to.

As a child of your heavenly Father, you are invited to communicate with Him through prayer. Prayer is easy – you simply share your heart with Him. He loves to answer your desires. Some good teachings on prayer will help you to grow in the many different ways that you can communicate with God. Prayer is very fulfilling and powerful.

All of God's goodness belongs to you when you are in Christ ... so imbibe of it all. You have been called to a full and glorious life in Jesus. Enjoy!

6

A DECREE

Proclaim this decree often over your life!

The Lord loves me with an everlasting love and has promised to give me a future and a hope. With lovingkindness, He has drawn me unto Himself. I look carefully and intently at the manner of love the Father has poured out upon me. It is through this love that He has called me to be His dear child. I am completely and fully accepted in Him, my God and Savior. Nothing can separate me from the love of God that is in Christ Jesus my Lord – not tribulation or distress, not persecution, famine or nakedness, not peril, sword, angels, principalities, powers, death, or life; neither things present nor things to come – absolutely nothing can separate me from the love of God which is in Christ Jesus my Lord.

God's love toward me is patient and kind. His love for me bears all things, believes all things, hopes all things and endures all things. His love will never fail. His love for me is so rich that He gave His only begotten Son. Because of this, I will never perish but have everlasting life with Him. As a result of God's great love for me, I have an unbreakable, eternal covenant with Him. Through this covenant of love, He has put His laws within my heart and written His commandments upon my mind.

I have been invited to the Lord's banqueting table, and His banner over me is love! His love is better than the choicest of wines. Through His intimate love, He draws me and invites me to follow after Him. I am fair and pleasant unto Him. I am rooted and grounded in His love, well able to comprehend with all believers the width and length and depth and height of His unfailing love. I have been called to know this rich love that surpasses knowledge so that I may be filled with all the fullness of God.

I truly am the object of God's deepest love and affection.

About Patricia King

Patricia King is a respected apostolic minister of the gospel and has been a pioneering voice in ministry, serving for over 30 years as a Christian minister in conference speaking, prophetic service, church leadership, and television and radio appearances. She is the founder of Patricia King Ministries, Women in Ministry Network and Patricia King Institute, the co-founder of XPmedia.com, and director of Women on the Frontlines. She has written many books, produced numerous CDs and DVDs, and hosts her TV program, *Supernatural Life*. She is also a successful business owner and an inventive entrepreneur. Patricia's reputation in the Christian community is world-renowned.

To Connect:

Patricia King website: PatriciaKing.com

Facebook: Facebook.com/PatriciaKingPage

Patricia King Institute: PatriciaKingInstitute.com

Women on the Frontlines and Women in Ministry Network: Wimnglobal.com

"Supernatural Life" TV show and many other video teachings by Patricia: XPmedia.com

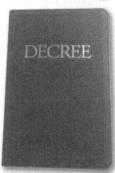
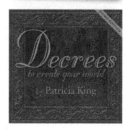

An Invitation to Spend Time with God

Sacred Time – Sacred Place, a Journal

This beautiful imitation leather journal has valuable tools to develop a rich devotional life. It includes practical guidelines to help you have a fruitful devotional time with Jesus, a plan to read the Bible in one year, and plenty of lined pages with a Bible Scripture at the bottom. Packaged in a gift box.

God's Law of Attraction

Your soul is the epicenter of what happens in your life.

Patricia King takes you on a riveting journey through your soul to discover why and, more importantly, how it holds the secret to a life of abundance and success. When your soul is aligned with God's promises and purposes, you can possess your destiny and live in the perpetual blessings of *God's Law of Attraction.*

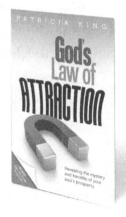